ST. PAUL: TEACHER

ST. PAUL: TEACHER AND TRAVELLER

Edited by

IVOR BULMER-THOMAS

THE FAITH PRESS
LEIGHTON BUZZARD, BEDS. LU7 7NQ

First published 1975
© *Ivor Bulmer-Thomas, 1975*

PRINTED IN GREAT BRITAIN
BY THE FAITH PRESS LTD.
LEIGHTON BUZZARD LU7 7NQ
SBN 7164 0415 X

CONTENTS

		Page
FOREWORD		9
1.	APOSTLE TO THE GENTILES *by* GERALD ELLISON	11
2.	ST. PAUL THE MAN *by* FRANCIS CLARK	17
3.	ST. PAUL'S CONVERSION *by* HAROLD WILSON	31
4.	ST. PAUL THE MISSIONARY *by* IVOR BULMER-THOMAS	36
	PART I. THE SOURCES	36
	PART II. ST. PAUL'S TRAVELS	42
5.	ST. PAUL'S SHIPWRECK *by* ANGUS ACWORTH	79
6.	ST. PAUL THE WRITER *by* COLIN HICKLING	85
7.	ST. PAUL ON GRACE *by* GORDON HUELIN	97
8.	ON BAPTISM AND THE SPIRIT *by* GEOFFREY LAMPE	107
9.	ON THE HOLY EUCHARIST *by* ERIC MASCALL	115
10.	ON THE UNITY OF THE CHURCH *by* HARRY CARPENTER	119
11.	ST. PAUL IN HISTORY *by* T. M. PARKER	125
INDEX		133

CONTRIBUTORS

The Rt. Revd. and Rt. Hon. Gerald Ellison, Lord Bishop of London

Dr. Francis Clark, Reader in Religious Studies, The Open University and Formerly Lecturer, The Gregorian University, Rome

The Revd. Canon Harold Wilson, Canon and Chancellor of St. Paul's Cathedral

Ivor Bulmer-Thomas, Superintendent, St. Andrew-by-the-Wardrobe Advanced Sunday School

Angus Acworth, Barrister-at-law and lately Hon. Treasurer, Georgian Group

The Revd. C. J. A. Hickling, Lecturer in New Testament Studies, University of London King's College, and Priest in Ordinary to H.M. The Queen

The Revd. Gordon Huelin, Guild Vicar of St. Margaret Pattens and Lecturer, King's College, London

The Revd. Professor Geoffrey Lampe, Regius Professor of Theology, University of Cambridge

The Revd. Canon Eric Mascall, Professor Emeritus of Historical Theology, University of London

The Rt. Revd. Harry Carpenter, lately Bishop of Oxford and co-Chairman of the Anglican-Orthodox Commission for Joint Doctrinal Discussions

The Revd. Thomas Maynard Parker, Fellow and lately Praelector in Theology and Modern History, University College, Oxford

FOREWORD

FOR the past ten years the church of St. Andrew-by-the-Wardrobe in the City of London has held during the winter an Advanced Sunday School at which leading speakers have introduced discussions of various aspects of the theme chosen for that season. Last year the theme was the inexhaustible subject of St. Paul—by any standard one of the most formative men in the history of the world, whether it be the world of thought or of action. The opening addresses were so good, that those who heard them thought they should be made available to a wider audience. The eminent scholars who took part readily agreed, and have re-written or revised their original texts in a manner suitable for publication. The result is this volume which it is hoped will be found acceptable as a study of the man and his work, his life and his letters, both by professed students of the subject and by the general public curious to know how within half a century the message of a Jewish teacher nailed to a tree had swept across the Roman world. This is the story of the man who, after being the chief persecutor of the Christians and experiencing a spectacular conversion, carried that message and interpreted it in a manner that still influences.

As editor of these essays I have had one disappointment. The original stimulating talk on "St. Paul the Missionary" was given by Mr. Stewart Perowne, but, having recently written a book on the subject—an excellent book, *The Journeys of St. Paul*—he did did not feel able to compose something new for this volume. The editor has therefore undertaken the task himself in his own way, but he is the first to regret that the thought and words are not those of Mr. Perowne.

In these days when a knowledge of the classical languages is not so widely diffused as it used to be we have thought it right to transliterate Greek words. After all, this has long been done for Hebrew and Aramaic, and is being increasingly done in works of scholarship. Scholars will, we hope, understand and those whose Greek is rusty or still to be learnt approve.

The editor has not sought to impose any uniformity upon his contributors—which would, indeed, be an impertinence with such a team—and he realizes that not all would agree with all his own conclusions. Where they touch upon the same topic there may be advantages in letting readers see how different scholars can come to different conclusions—for example, on the dating of *Acts* and the letters, or the authenticity of some of the letters—in fields where complete certainty on the present evidence is unattainable. In one feature we all agree: whether our conclusions are judged revolutionary or conservative (and what was conservative a generation ago may now be revolutionary) our methods are those of critical scholarship. Some of us who call ourselves Catholic (one would not deny the title Roman Catholic), some Evangelical, and probably most of us would claim to be both Catholic and Evangelical: so was St. Paul, who has brought us together.

The mosaic portrait of St. Paul used as a frontispiece is regarded by Walter Oakeshott in *The Mosaics of Rome* (where it is reproduced in colour, Plate III) as a fragment from the original Constantinian apsidal mosaic in the old basilica of St. Peter, Rome (pp. 67–70). If so—and there seems every reason to accept the attribution—it is of mid-fourth century date and is the oldest known representation of St. Paul. It is now in the Vatican grottoes. The photograph is reproduced by the kind permission of the owner of the copyright, Scala editions of Florence.

IVOR BULMER-THOMAS

12 Edwardes Square,
London W8 6HG
11th April 1975

CHAPTER I

APOSTLE TO THE GENTILES

by
Gerald Ellison

I SUPPOSE that, on any computation, St. Paul is one of the most remarkable men who have ever lived. He is almost unique, not only in the extent of his influence, but also in the amount we know about him; indeed he is one of the few figures that stand out from antiquity with a clarity which can be assured comes from real and genuine sources of information. We know about him from writings of St. Luke, in the *Acts;* we know about him from his own self-revelation in his letters. From these sources we are entitled to form a clear picture of this remarkable figure that dominates so much of human history. And it may well be claimed that that domination dates from the experience which he underwent on the Damascus road, which is so well documented for us both in the account in the *Acts* and also in the personal testimony about his experience given by St. Paul himself. The facts are well known and need no embroidery: he was going down to Damascus, riding with an armed guard, with the deliberate intent of seeking out and destroying those who were followers of Christ; and there he underwent the sudden and tremendous spiritual and physical experience which has become the *locus classicus* for the experience of sudden conversion.

Though this may be the most remarkable recorded manifestation of this phenomenon in Christian history, we know, of course, that it is not unique. There have been other instances of what one may call sudden conversion. St. Francis underwent a moment of sudden conversion when at a particular moment he got off his horse and bent down and kissed the leper. John Wesley underwent an experience of sudden conversion when at a place not so very far from this spot* he experienced a strange warming of his heart

---

*[The address on which this essay is based was given at the church of St. Andrew-by-the-Wardrobe in the City of London on the Feast of the Epiphany, 6th January 1974; it was at a meeting in Aldersgate Street in the City that Wesley's heart was "strangely warmed" on 24th May 1738. —Ed.]

and this very ordinary and not particularly successful Anglican clergyman became the first person from whom flowed out all the power and initiative of the Methodist movement. St. Paul's conversion is therefore comparable in its suddenness with other experiences; and it is also comparable in that it is pretty clear that although certain people do undergo this sudden and violent experience, it is seldom *de novo*, it is seldom an experience that comes out of nothing. It is rather the accumulation of a great deal of heart searching, of suffering, of longing for the truth, and of bewilderment, which culminate at a particular moment, when a man is stopped in his tracks and turned round and set on a new way. We may be quite sure that this experience of St. Paul was the climax of a long period of personal spiritual upheaval. We know that he was brought up a very strict and devout Jew and that he was deeply devoted to the synagogue and all that it represented. We know that he had seen the dangers—as he and the orthodox church considered them—of this strange new movement within the Jewish Church. For one must remember that at the time of his conversion, as far as we are told, the name "Christian" had not been given to this group of people who shared a particular interpretation of Jewish history and theology, who believed in a strange new teaching about the hope that was in the life of every Jew, and who he and the leaders of the church believed must be eradicated. We know that he had been a senior witness at the martyrdom of St. Stephen and that he was given a commission to go and seek out and to destroy Christians wherever they were to be found. And one can presume that during this period there was a psychological process, familiar to many people, going on within him. He had seen something which he knew was an answer to the hopes and fears and complications of his own spiritual life, which he knew would make great demands upon him, of which he was consequently afraid, and from which he sought to withdraw by eradicating it. He wanted to destroy the thing which he knew he ought to love; he wanted to kill the people whom secretly in his own heart he envied because he knew that they had got something he needed, something which, therefore, he must either accept or reject. It must have been this turmoil of spiritual experience which was going on in his soul when he accepted the office of being a chief persecutor of the Christians.

On the journey to Damascus he would have passed through a great many places which were already hallowed by experiences of personal contact with Jesus. The situation was therefore ripe for the great spiritual experience that awaited him. And so, on the road to Damascus, there was the sudden light, the violent physical experience of being thrown from his horse and falling to the ground, and the clear voice as he came face to face with Jesus, who challenged him and who spoke to him and who set his life on a new road. That moment was of course to have immense consequences for himself. It certainly was not to lead to peace and to ease of life. It was to drive him out into the physical dangers of widespread travel in the ancient world. It was to subject him to physical pain and persecution, such as that recorded in 2 *Corinthians* 11. It was to mean for him the bitter experience, as one must surmise, of losing many of his closest friends and of finding himself rejected from the worship of the synagogue, which had meant so much to him and which had been a very part and parcel of his own life. It was to mean, perhaps above all, the pain of the care of all the churches. There is surely nothing more moving than the recorded accounts in his letters of the way in which those who had the greatest debt to him, the people who owed him more than anything, could turn against him, could criticize him, could reject or misunderstand the very heart of the gospel that he had come to offer to them. Those who have ever been on a pilgrimage to the middle east will no doubt have gone to the site of Corinth. It is one of the most moving of all the sacred sites, for now is but a pile of stones where once stood a great and thriving city. This is the place where you can walk up the street where St. Paul's own feet have trod. This is the place where presumably 1 *Corinthians* 13 was first heard by Christian people. And yet, here were the people who derided St. Paul, who criticized him, not only for his teaching but for his bearing and for his personal characteristics, and it was to them that he had to eat humble pie, to them he had to justify himself. There is nothing more touching than the way in which so many who owed St Paul everything in the spiritual sense so misunderstood him and caused him so much pain and distress. But despite all these sufferings, what happened on the Damascus road brought to Paul the sense of spiritual peace, the satisfaction, the understanding, the experience of God which the Jewish Law had denied him.

The conversion of St. Paul was also, of course, a deeply satisfying event for the young Christian Church, if indeed we are entitled yet to call it such. It is clear that there was a very real danger that in those early days the group of believers could have, to use Evelyn Underhill's phrase, "twisted in its tracks", have gone wrong, have developed merely as one small sect within the Jewish church, a sect which had a peculiar belief about the fulfilment of the hope of Israel. And it was the conversion of St. Paul which rescued the Christian Church and gave it its power and its initiative. Can one imagine the joy that must have come to the early Christians, who believed that they were almost certainly faced with annihilation, who were being pursued and ferreted out and destroyed, at the moment when the amazing news filtered through that the one person who had above all been leading the chase, the arch persecutor himself, had suddenly seen the light and had confessed himself the disciple of Jesus? St. Paul's conversion, therefore, must be counted one of the great events of history because it rescued the early Church, gave it an identity, and charted its course in a direction that allowed it to grow into the Christian Church as we see it throughout the world today.

The conversion of St. Paul, indeed, is the significant event which gives theological meaning to the whole doctrine of salvation as he expounded it: it is his teaching, his insight, which saw that the Christian gospel was for all men and that if Jesus died for any he died for all. He, of course, felt that it was his duty first of all to preach the gospel to the Jews. Wherever he went on his missionary journeys, his first call was on the synagogue. But the formative moment came at Antioch in Pisidia where, having been persecuted and having been misunderstood in the synagogue, he announced proudly that he was turning to the Gentiles. It is through his teaching that the new covenant was recognized, that the new Israel is the Christian Church, that it has been possible for the gospel to be preached to all men and the new Israel to be proclaimed as enclosing the whole of the human race.

There are of course those who contend that St. Paul made the Christian faith more difficult and more complicated: that he debased the pure coinage of the teaching of Jesus, and that if only we had been left with the gospels and the person and example of Jesus, then everything would have been so much easier. Of course the reverse is almost the truth: St. Paul was, so to speak, the cross-roads from which the light of the gospel, because of his particular personality and understanding, shone forth in so many directions. Because he was a Jew versed in the teaching of the synagogue he understood the nature of the law and, from his own experience, the constrictions which it placed upon him, the barrier it was setting up between man and God. As someone who had been born in Tarsus he understood the prevailing Greek philosophy and frame of mind and was therefore able to interpret the Christian Gospel to the philosophical attitudes of his time. As a Roman citizen he had access to the world-wide influence of the

Roman Empire. And his appeal to Caesar, his being sent to Rome, meant that he went to the very heart of the communications of the known civilized world and that therefore the teaching which he was able to give to the disciples was centred in some place where it could, and perhaps could alone in the ancient world, have broken out and spread. Much of the history of mankind flows from the conversion of this fascinating character, about whom we know so much, both from his letters, and from the devoted biography of that wonderfully self-effacing friend St. Luke. I always think that there is no more pathetic cry and yet no more splendid tribute to loyalty and devotion than the words of the captive Paul from Rome, "Only Luke is with me". It is he who must have borne with all the tempestuous outbursts and yet the warm-hearted friendship of the man to whom he devoted so much of his life. I don't think I can sum up what St. Paul ought to mean to all of us better than by quoting a longish passage from a book which has always meant a great deal to me, although it was written a very long time ago. Some of you may be admirers of the work of S. C. Carpenter who was for a long time master of the Temple down the road here and then Dean of Exeter. He can write Christian history so that it reads like a novel, and he can also expound the Bible in a way which brings life and vitality and relevance to the events and to the people who we read about in its pages. In a book called *The Bible View of Life* he has a chapter entitled "The Burning Heart" which comes from the passage in the twenty-fourth chapter of St. Luke: "Did not our heart burn within us as he talked with us by the way and while he opened to us the scriptures?"; and the purpose of the chapter is to examine certain people and see how they open to us the scriptures: I am therefore, in closing, going to read this passage to you because, as I say, it sets out what St. Paul ought to mean to us more clearly than any words that I could utter: He says:

"St. Paul is far and away the most interesting character in history. A shepherd of souls and an organizing genius, a man of many friends, a gentleman, warm-hearted, irritable, tender and affectionate, yet cast in heroic mould, combining to an astonishing degree humility and courage, courtesy and resolution, passion and common sense. Passages of his letters are as eloquent as anything ever written, and yet he is never trying to be eloquent. A brutal critic has suggested that Shakespeare's plays were pot-boilers. St. Paul's Epistles are not even pot-boilers. They are his casual conversation, his remarks at meals, the house-to-house greetings of a parish priest. But open some standard commentary like

Sanday and Headlam's *Romans*, and see their list of 'detached notes'. In a few cases the titles are technical and unfamiliar, but the topics are those of to-day and every day. Think of a man whose essay of a few hundred words, written in spare moments, and, so to speak, in trains and waiting rooms and omnibuses, is the *locus classicus* on the relation between Faith and Conduct, the Righteousness of God, Justification, the meaning of the Old Testament, the Fall of Man, the doctrine of mystical union with Christ, the Renovation of Nature, Election, the Power and Rights of God, as Creator, Predestination, and Free Will. A man whose ineradicable Hebraism gave him a true outlook upon life, whose Greek environment and command of the Greek language made him the creator of Christian theological terminology, whose Roman citizenship gave him his dream of a Christian Empire. A man who could wither the Corinthians with the only weapon that ever pierces spiritual pride, and yet call them, as indeed they were, his beloved saints. A man who could write *Philippians* and *Ephesians* and *Philemon*. A man who had resisted conviction, as we all do, for years, and then faced the humiliation of admitting that his whole previous life had been a gigantic error, who endured incalculable hardships and disappointments, and the loss of every friend and relation that he had. All this without a groan, without even a murmur. Why? Because he once saw Jesus, whom he had persecuted, and there and then laid his whole being at his feet" (S. C. Carpenter, *The Bible View of Life* (London, Eyre and Spottiswoode, 1937), pp. 183–184).

On a day when we are bidden to follow the example of the wise men and lay our gifts at the feet of the infant Christ, a day when we celebrate the showing forth of Christ to the Gentiles, whom better on this day can we honour than St. Paul?

CHAPTER II

ST. PAUL THE MAN*

by

Francis Clark

WE are to study the life, deeds, writings and achievements of Paul of Tarsus, one of the most remarkable religious teachers in the history of mankind. As sources for this study we shall use, as well as the account of Paul's activity given in *The Acts of the Apostles*, the corpus of Pauline letters. Some later apocryphal writings offer further particulars about his life, but their value as historical sources is practically negligible. It is just possible that they contain some grains of remembered fact amidst the legendary chaff—for instance in the description of Paul's personal appearance given in the *Acts of Paul and Thecla*, dating from the later second century: "A man small of stature, with a bald head and crooked legs, in a good state of body, with eyebrows meeting and nose somewhat hooked, full of friendliness".[1] These facial characteristics are in fact found in representations of Paul in Christian art from the fourth century onwards.

Of the thirteen Pauline letters, it is widely agreed that at least nine, and probably ten, were personally written by Paul, or at least dictated by him to amanuenses. (A fourteenth letter, *Hebrews*, was for long ascribed to Paul, but it is clearly by another author.) Many scholars do not accept the Pauline authorship of the so-called "Pastoral Letters"—namely, the two letters to *Timothy* and the letter to *Titus*, which they think date from a rather later time. Some scholars, while admitting that the letter to the *Ephesians* reflects authentically Pauline ideas, also doubt whether it is directly from Paul. Here and there in his letters Paul makes incidental autobiographical references, and from these, coupled with the data given in *Acts* and from the enduring evidence of his achieve-

---

* This chapter incorporates material which is also contained, in amplified form, in a coursebook written by the author, entitled *The Rise of Christianity* (The Open University Press, 1973). Grateful acknowledgement is made to the Open University Press for the use of this material.

[1] Hennecke-Schneemelcher, *New Testament Apocrypha* (London, 1965), Vol. 2, p. 354.

ments in the churches he founded or instructed, we can piece together something like a "life" of Paul. Most useful for biographical data of this kind are his letters to the *Romans*, his two letters to the *Corinthians*, and his letters to the *Galatians* and *Philippians*.

We do not always find a neat agreement between *Acts* and Paul's letters on points of fact, and there are many tantalizing ambiguities and gaps in the story. But in spite of—indeed, because of—those discordances, the substantial agreement of the two sources about the main lines of Paul's life, ministry and achievements is impressive. We can have a fair measure of confidence that our historical knowledge of this remarkable man is at least as accurate as our knowledge of most of the other great figures of antiquity. Indeed it has been fairly said that of all the characters of antiquity none except Cicero is so intimately known to us as Paul of Tarsus. There is a limpid consistency in the unintended self-portrait of Paul which emerges from his surviving letters, in which he pours out his impetuous thoughts and aspirations.

There are disputes among scholars about the problem of fitting the autobiographical particulars gleaned from Paul's letters into the pattern of Paul's missionary journeys given in *Acts*. There is no time to enter into the details of these disputes here. Given the fragmentary nature of the evidence and the theological *genre* of the writings under consideration, we do not expect them to provide a tidy historical picture. Luke's account, though partly based, it would seem, on a travel diary which he himself kept while in Paul's company, is patently not an exact log of all the journeys Paul made during the more than twenty years, nor can it be a complete record of all places, dates and travel-schedules in the story. Moreover, Paul's own references in his letters to his travels and doings are usually recollections put in to illustrate some point of pastoral concern in his argument. Instead of following the more usual pattern, which divides Paul's public ministry into three well-defined missionary journeys, I suggest that we group the data from our sources in a rather more general survey. It is well not to be too preoccupied with identifying and numbering individual "journeys" in the career of a man whose life was one long restless series of "journeyings often". As he himself summed it up: "I have been constantly on the road; I have met dangers from rivers, dangers from robbers, dangers from my fellow-countrymen, dangers from foreigners, dangers in towns, dangers in the country, dangers at sea, dangers from false friends" (*2 Cor.* 11: 26). I will give under five headings an outline of the main phases in

Paul's life, indicating the principal places in which he was active, and the churches which he founded or with which he was associated.

(1) *Paul's early life up to his "conversion"*

Born at Tarsus, the principal city of Cilicia, the son of a pious family of Diaspora Jews, Paul—whose Jewish name was Saul—could thus refer to his antecedents: "Circumcised on my eighth day, Israelite by race, of the tribe of Benjamin, a Hebrew born and bred; in my attitude to the law, a Pharisee; in pious zeal, a persecutor of the church, in legal rectitude, faultless" (*Phil.* 3: 5–6). His father, doubtless a tent-maker by profession as Paul was in his turn, had, rather surprisingly, the coveted privilege of Roman citizenship, a hereditary advantage which his son was able to put to good use in emergencies. Staunchly loyal though he was to the traditions of his race, Saul also had a civic pride in his native city: "I am a Jew, a Tarsian from Cilicia, a citizen of no mean city" (*Acts* 21: 39). Tarsus was a fairly large port at a cross-roads of international trade, renowned for its textiles. It was also a centre of Hellenistic culture, claiming to rival even Athens and Alexandria in its fame for learning. Paul was a child of two cultures. While his Jewish spiritual heritage was the most formative influence, he also knew the ways of the Hellenistic world. While he came from Aramaic-speaking forebears and spoke that language fluently (cf. *Acts* 21: 40), he also acquired fluent and flexible use of the *koinē* Greek which was to be the medium of his apostolate and of his epistles. He knew the Greek Septuagint version of the Jewish Scriptures through and through, and his own writing was to be impregnated with its phrases.

According to *Acts* 22: 3, Paul declared that although born in Tarsus he had been brought up in Jerusalem, "and as a pupil of Gamaliel I was thoroughly trained in every point of our ancestral law". In *Galatians* 1: 14 Paul describes "how in the practice of our national religion I was outstripping many of my Jewish contemporaries in my boundless devotion to the traditions of my ancestors". When did Paul go to Jerusalem to study? Possibly as a child; he had relatives in Judaea (*Acts* 23: 16). His advanced studies at the feet of the highly-reputed Gamaliel would have been undertaken before (or possibly even after) the years of Christ's public ministry, for Paul never mentions seeing or hearing of Jesus Christ during his mortal life. From his rabbinical studies Paul acquired mental agility, subtlety in scriptural interpretation, the ardent zeal of the Pharisees, and a deepening of his sense of complete religious dedication to God.

The first mention of Paul in *Acts* is to describe his presence at the stoning of Stephen (7: 58 – 8: 1). That Paul took an active part in persecution of the infant Christian Church is confirmed by his repeated avowals in his letters (e.g. *1 Cor.* 15: 9; *Gal.* 1: 13; *Phil.* 3: 6). According to *Acts*, it was while he was on his way to Damascus, "breathing murderous threats against the disciples of the Lord" and planning to bring them back captive to Jerusalem, that the whole course of his life was changed by a supernatural intervention of the risen Christ (9: 1–19). The same extraordinary episode, with substantially the same circumstances, is twice more related in *Acts* (22: 4–11 and 26: 12–18). In his letters Paul does not mention the particulars of the blinding experience on the Damascus road, but he does make definite allusions to a decisive encounter with the risen Christ, and to being changed by God's grace from a persecutor into an Apostle (*1 Cor.* 9: 1; 15: 8–10; *Gal.* 1: 11–12; *Phil.* 3: 12). In *Galatians* 1: 13–17, Paul affirms that God revealed his Son to him while he was actively engaged in persecuting the Church, and he explicitly associates the happening with Damascus, to which he "afterwards returned". Whatever the precise circumstances, and whatever the possible explanation of the apparition or revelation, both *Acts* and Paul's own letters are in substantial agreement in attributing his conversion to Christianity to a sudden and direct divine intervention. Assuming that the crucifixion of Jesus occurred about the year 30, the martyrdom of Stephen can be dated about AD 33, and Paul's conversion would be about a year later.

(2) *The period of reorientation, and Paul's subsequent mission, based on Antioch, to the southern regions of Asia Minor*

Acts records that Paul's sight was miraculously restored at Damascus by a disciple named Ananias, and that he was then baptized (9: 10–19). Paul was now gripped with a burning conviction that dictated the whole future course of his life. The crucified Galilean whose followers he had been persecuting was not the imposter he had supposed. Jesus of Nazareth was the Messiah and the living Lord who had called his adversary to his service. Paul himself recalled that after the supernatural revelation which revolutionized his life he "went off at once to Arabia" (*Gal.* 1: 17), no doubt to meditate upon what had happened and what it meant. Hitherto he had been intent on meriting God's favour by meticulous devotion to the Jewish Law; now he was overwhelmed by the realization that in his greatest zeal he had been meriting, not reward, but divine wrath and punishment. And yet he had been chosen for God's favour while he was God's enemy. Thenceforward he was to be the herald of God's "free grace". After the period of retirement in the desert Paul returned to Damascus (*Gal.* 1: 17). *Acts* is silent about the Arabian interlude, but relates that Paul preached his new-found faith with great energy in Damascus, thus provoking for the first time that hostile reaction from the Jews which he was to encounter everywhere. Our two sources agree that he was in mortal peril at Damascus, and that he escaped by being lowered over the city wall in a basket (*Acts* 9: 23–5; *2 Cor.* 11: 32–3).

Three years afterwards (about AD 36–37) Paul went up to Jerusalem "to get to know Cephas", that is, Peter. He later recalled that he stayed with Peter for a fortnight and also saw James, the brother of Jesus, but otherwise did not mix with the Christians in Judaea (*Gal.* 1: 18–24). The account in *Acts* 9: 26–30 differs from Paul's in some particulars. Luke says the brethren in Jerusalem were all afraid of Paul, but Barnabas, a Cypriot who had handed over his wealth to the Church's common chest, befriended Paul and introduced him to the apostles. Paul then moved about freely in Jerusalem, preaching the gospel of Jesus and debating with Hellenistic Jews. When danger arose the brethren escorted Paul safely away.

Paul's zeal soon brought him into further danger. He withdrew from Judaea "to the regions of Syria and Cilicia", returning to his native city of Tarsus (*Gal.* 1: 21; *Acts* 9: 30). He seems to have spent several years (from about 37 to 44) in those regions. The Judaean congregations heard reports of his evangelistic ardour and praised God for it (*Gal.* 1: 23). It was during those years, to judge from *2 Cor.* 12: 1–10, that he underwent an ecstatic experience which profoundly affected him. He also contracted a humiliating physical disability which was to remain with him through later years. Eventually Barnabas went to Tarsus to seek out Paul, with the aim of bringing him to share in the work of the gospel at Antioch, now a principal centre of Christian activity. Antioch, with its port Seleucia at the mouth of the Orontes, was a wealthy and populous centre of communications and commerce. It was the capital of the Roman province of Syria. At Antioch "the disciples first got the name of Christians", and it was there too that significant numbers of Gentiles first became converts. From Antioch

Paul and Barnabas visited Jerusalem to take "famine relief" to the needy Christians (*Acts* 11: 25–31).

It was probably between the years 45 and 48 that Paul and Barnabas were active in the southern regions of Asia Minor. Luke relates how they were solemnly commissioned for this task by leading members of the Antioch congregation, and in chapters 13–14 of *Acts* he tells the story of their missionary travels, first in Cyprus, then in Pamphylia and in cities in the southern part of the province of Galatia—Pisidian Antioch, Iconium, Lystra and Derbe. Luke's record of the places evangelized is doubtless not complete, for he remarks that "the word of the Lord spread far and wide through the region" (*Acts* 13: 49).

The description of events at Pisidian Antioch gives a good illustration of how Paul normally introduced the gospel by preaching first to the Diaspora Jews and proselytes in the local synagogue, and then to a wider circle of interested Gentiles outside. The sermon here attributed to Paul in the synagogue is similar to others in which Luke sums up the early apostolic preaching about the risen Christ. He also relates the retort given by Paul and Barnabas to the Galatian Jews who rejected the Christian message, in words which could serve as a statement of Luke's own editorial theme: "It was necessary that the word of God should be declared to you first. But since you reject it and thus condemn yourselves as unworthy of eternal life, we now turn to the Gentiles. For these are our instructions from the Lord: 'I have appointed you to be a light for the Gentiles and a means of salvation to earth's farthest bounds'" (*Acts* 13: 46–7). Inevitably persecution arose, but many Gentiles were converted. Luke adds a comment which is reminiscent of a key theme in Paul's letters: "Those who were marked out for eternal life became believers". Though subjected to physical violence, the missionaries founded fervent congregations in the places they visited, and appointed "elders" in each. Returning to Antioch, they reported "how God had thrown open the gates of faith to the Gentiles" (*Acts* 14: 27).

(3) *Paul's missionary activity in Macedonia and central Greece*

According to *Acts*, the great dispute about the observance of the ritual prescriptions of the Jewish Law, and about what obligations should be laid on the Gentile Christians, came to a head at this point in the story and was resolved at what is often called the "Council of Jerusalem". However, the allusions to the controversy in Paul's letters show that it was not settled so unambiguously and finally at that time. At least it is clear that both *Acts* and *Galatians* 2 agree that the liberal policy of Paul and Barnabas towards the Gentile converts was vindicated by a meeting in Jerusalem, at which leading members of the apostolic community, in particular, Peter and James the brother of Jesus, recognized the correctness of Paul's attitude. This controversy with the "Judaizers" was to beset Paul's apostolate for many years.

Paul realized that the chief places of government, culture and trade in the Roman empire were the most advantageous for the purpose of spreading the gospel. In the next main phase of his missionary activity, as described in *Acts*, his prime objective was the Roman province of proconsular Asia. This populous region facing the Aegean Sea had several busy ports and a prosperous hinterland. Ephesus, the metropolis of the province, was the start of a great Roman road to the east; a main line of communication from the east to Rome led westwards from Ephesus across the Aegean and the Adriatic, *via* Corinth. Landward routes to Europe ran from the north-west of the province across the Hellespont. On his first attempt to reach this important region Paul, who had now parted company from Barnabas, was diverted from his intended route. After passing through Syria and Cilicia and revisiting the places in southern Galatia which he had earlier evangelized with Barnabas, he was "prevented by the Holy Spirit from delivering the message in the province of Asia" (*Acts* 16: 6). Instead he and his new companion Silas made their way through Phrygia and probably through north Galatia. Again, according to Luke, a supernatural premonition directed their steps away from Bithynia and towards the sea coast of Troas, near the Hellespont. Here a nocturnal vision beckoned Paul across into Europe. His party now included Timothy, a keen young convert from Lystra, and—to judge from the "we-passages" in *Acts,* which begin at this point in the narrative—Luke himself.

Paul's ministry in Macedonia and Greece was attended with notable success, as well as with some failures and the usual persecutions. The first congregation he founded in Europe was at Philippi; it was always to be especially dear to him. Others were founded at Thessalonica and Beroea. Then he went on to Athens, where, despite his efforts to suit his message to the sophisticated audience, he achieved little. We hear of individual Athenian converts, but of no continuing church there during Paul's lifetime. When he went on to Corinth, on the other hand, he found many people ready to listen to the message of a religion very different from that of Corinthian Aphrodite, with her thousand temple prostitutes. He made a fairly long stay there, probably about two years, and planted a church which was to have an important place in early Christian history. His ministry was not confined to Corinth; we learn from *Romans* 16: 1 that there was a church in the nearby port of Cenchreae. In these Greek cities, as in Asia Minor, Paul preached first in the synagogues, then in public to the Gentiles as well. We find several references to pious and influential women converts. In Corinth the usual violent opposition was stirred up against him and his companions. Because of this hostility we have one of our few fixed points of reference in New Testament chronology. It was the action of the Corinthian Jews in bringing Paul before the tribunal of Gallio, proconsul of Achaia and brother of the philosopher Seneca, that enables us to date Paul's stay in that city fairly accurately, in the years 51–52 or 52–53.

Luke relates that Paul left Corinth some time after that episode, making his way to Caesarea and Jerusalem, in order to "pay his respects to the church" and perhaps to fulfil a vow in the Temple (*Acts* 18: 18–22). In the years that followed, his congregations in Macedonia and Achaia were constantly in his thoughts. His concern for them is apparent in the letters he addressed to them, some of which survive—two to the Thessalonians, two to the Corinthians, one to the Philippians. The problems of the restless Corinthian congregation caused him particular anxiety. There are references in his letters to further travels in Macedonia and to a sudden extra visit to Corinth. In *Acts* 20 Luke describes a later visit to Macedonia and then a stay of three months in Greece, followed by a return to Philippi for the Passover season. These travels can be dated approximately between the years 55 and 57. There was also a visit to Illyricum (a region roughly corresponding to the modern Yugoslavia), alluded to in *Romans* 15: 19 but otherwise unrecorded.

(4) *The Ephesus phase: Paul's ministry in proconsular Asia*

Paul's first visit to Ephesus was a short one. *Acts* 18 : 19–21 tells how he visited the city on his way from Corinth to Caesarea, which would have been about the year 52 or 53. He preached in the synagogue there, but when the Jews of the city urged him to make a longer stay, he declined, saying, "I shall come back to you if it is God's will". A year or so later he at last found the way open to achieve his ambition of preaching the gospel in proconsular Asia. From his old base at Antioch he set out, first revisiting the congregations in Galatia and Phrygia, "bringing new strength to all the converts" (*Acts* 18: 23). Then, unhindered this time by any providential dissuasion, he was able to travel through the highlands of Anatolia to reach Ephesus. He made Ephesus his headquarters for about three years—his longest and most successful ministry in any one place. Luke even asserts that as a result of his preaching "the whole population of the province of Asia, both Jews and pagans, heard the word of the Lord" (*Acts* 19: 10). It must have been during this period that the gospel was spread to the cities of Colossae, Laodicea and Hierapolis by Epaphras, Paul's emissary, whom he called "a trusted worker for Christ on our behalf" (cf. *Col.* 1: 7; 4: 12–14). It was from Ephesus that Paul wrote his first letter to the Corinthians (cf. *1 Cor.* 16: 9).

After the first three months in Ephesus Jewish opposition made it impossible for Paul to preach in the synagogue, so he withdrew his converts and took over a lecture hall, where he discoursed daily. Luke records that he performed miracles and exorcisms, whereupon the whole population of the city was awestruck. Many renounced their magical practices, "and the name of the Lord Jesus gained in honour". Even "some dignitaries of the province were friendly to Paul". So successful was he in winning men and women over to the Christian way of life that the cult of the goddess Artemis, which was big business in Ephesus, suffered severe loss. This provoked the serious riot which threw the city into an uproar (*Acts* 19: 23–41). Some scholars argue that Paul suffered an imprisonment, unrecorded in *Acts*, during this (or a later) stay in Ephesus, and that the so-called "Letters of the Captivity" (*Philippians, Colossians, Ephesians* and *Philemon*) were written from there. The more usual opinion, however, is that these letters were written during Paul's imprisonment in Rome, or, less probably, in Caesarea.

It was soon after the riot that Paul left Ephesus to resume his travels in Macedonia and Greece. On his return journey, bound for Jerusalem, he purposely avoided Ephesus, summoning the elders of the Ephesian church to meet him at Miletus. In the expectation that they would never see his face again, he renewed his pastoral instructions and exhorted them: "Keep watch over yourselves and over all the flock of which the Holy Spirit has given you charge, as shepherds of the church of the Lord, which he won for himself by his own blood" (*Acts* 20: 15-38). All the same, it is not unlikely that Paul did go back to Ephesus again.

(5) *The climax of Acts: from Jerusalem to Rome*

The last eight chapters of *Acts* are an account of the climax of Paul's life, as Luke saw it at the time of writing. There is a mounting sense of drama as the Apostle makes his way, amid gloomy forebodings, from Corinth to Palestine, where tribulations and threats to his life await him. The tension rises again as he journeys from Palestine, through further perils and hardships, towards his ultimate goal—Rome. These chapters make up over half of what Luke tells us about the career of Paul. There is a kind of parallelism here to the account of the life of Jesus given in the Gospels, where the last phase in hostile Jerusalem is the most important part of the story. In Chapters 21–26 of *Acts* Luke emphasizes how Paul bore his witness in Jerusalem and later in Caesarea, and how high-ranking Roman officials found again and again that no just accusation lay against him. When Paul made his "appeal to Caesar" at the tribunal of the governor Porcius Festus at Caesarea (*Acts* 25: 11–12), his bold move made possible what for a long time he had yearned to achieve—to preach the good news of Jesus in the imperial capital itself. When setting out on his last journey from Corinth to Jerusalem he had written to the Roman Christians telling them of his "eagerness to declare the gospel in Rome as well as to others", and how he had often planned to go there, but so far without success (*Rom.* 1: 11–15; *cf.* also *Acts* 19: 21; *2 Cor.* 10: 16). Now he is going to bear his witness in the centre of the world stage, in Rome itself. According to *Acts*, while Paul was in mortal danger in Jerusalem the Lord Jesus appeared to him in a vision and said: "Keep up your courage; you have affirmed the truth about me in Jerusalem, and you must do the same in Rome" (23: 11).

So Paul is sent to Rome under military guard, accompanied by some faithful disciples, including Luke himself. Finally, after a perilous sea voyage (graphically narrated by Luke in a chapter which is not only a gripping adventure story but also a main source of our knowledge about ancient seamanship), Paul reaches Rome. There he spends two years (until about AD 62) under a kind of house arrest, "proclaiming the kingdom of God and teaching the facts about the Lord Jesus Christ quite openly and without hindrance". These are the last words of *Acts*. The book thus ends enigmatically, without telling us what befell Paul after his two years' stay in Rome. Several suggestions have been advanced to explain this strange ending to the book. The simplest explanation is that *Acts* was written at the end of Paul's two-year period in Rome, so that the author could not say what happened later. This theory is logically separable from the further suggestion that *Luke–Acts* were written as a vindication of Paul to help him in his defence before the Roman authorities.

When writing to the Romans at the end of his final visit to Corinth, Paul had declared his intention, after visiting Rome, of pressing on to Spain; he had been longing to go there for many years (*Rom.* 15: 23, 28). His missionary strategy, as explained in *2 Corinthians* 10: 14–16, was to take as his "proper sphere" Gentile regions which had not been evangelized by others. When he had completed his work in the eastern half of the Mediterranean world he would go to the west. "Then", he told the Corinthians, "we can carry the gospel to lands that lie beyond you". Paul was a man of iron perseverance and never lost sight of objectives he had resolved upon. If indeed he was acquitted at the imperial tribunal in Rome, and released from surveillance after his two years' stay in the city, it would have been quite unlike him not to pursue his plan to go on westwards in order to spread the gospel in Spain, where other men had not yet laid foundations for it. At the end of the first century the *Letter of Clement of Rome* affirms that Paul "preached in the east and in the west . . . and reached the farthest limits of the west"—which seems to mean Spain. In the same source there are also indications that Paul was later martyred in Rome; thus the author implies that Paul left the city after the stay recorded in *Acts* and returned there at some later time.

Some scholars think that Paul went back to Asia Minor during the years following the date at which *Acts* end. There are passages in the letters to *Timothy* and to *Titus,* which seem to refer to a period of Paul's life and activity subsequent to that covered by *Acts.* Whether these Pastoral Epistles were actually written by Paul himself or not, they may at least be taken as indicating an early belief that Paul had a further period in freedom after his first Roman captivity, and that he was subsequently imprisoned again, with the expectation of death before him (cf. *2 Tim.* 2: 9; 4: 6–8).

There seems good reason to accept the tradition that Paul suffered martyrdom in Rome during the reign of Nero. There are many indications, both literary and archaeological, from the post-apostolic period which converge to make it very probable that both Peter and Paul were put to death in Rome during the Neronian persecution. Although the site of St. Paul's reputed tomb under the basilica that bears his name has not yet been scientifically excavated, the constant local tradition relating to his martyrdom and burial is as strong as that relating to St. Peter's. There is evidence going back to the second century that the tomb of St. Paul was honoured in a roadside cemetery near the Ostian gate of the city. The place of his martyrdom was pointed out at *Aquae Salviae* on the Via Laurentina, which branches off from the road to Ostia.

(6) *The place of Paul in the early Church*

There is a unity of design running through the two-volume work which is made up by *Luke–Acts*. The life, death and resurrection of Jesus Christ, narrated in St. Luke's Gospel, are the foundation; the primitive Christianity of the Jerusalem church, described in the first dozen chapters of *Acts*, rises on that foundation; and this primitive Christianity of Jerusalem authorizes and validates the mission to the Gentiles, for which the Apostle Paul is set apart by a unique divine choice. The author of *Acts* thus demonstrates that Paul's ministry is duly linked with that of the body of the twelve accredited apostles who were entrusted by Jesus with the planting and spreading of the Kingdom of God. But he also shows that Paul is not just a secondary figure, a later convert sent out by the original apostles as their delegate. No, by a supernatural intervention on the Damascus road he is directly marked out by the risen Jesus himself, and suddenly changed from being a persecutor into an apostle of the first rank, entrusted with the widest mission of all: "This man is my chosen instrument to bring my name before the nations and their kings, and before the people of Israel. I myself will show him all that he must go through for my name's sake" (*Acts* 9: 15–16). In his letters Paul insisted that he was "an apostle, not by human appointment or human commission, but by commission from Jesus Christ and from God the Father who raised him from the dead" (*Gal.* 1: 1).

There was something ambivalent in Paul's relationship with the other leaders and missioners in the early Church, and in his attitude to the parent church in Palestine. The Jerusalem brethren recognized Paul as an authentic minister of the gospel and as a successful colleague in the service of Christ—yet at times it seemed to be an almost grudging recognition. Paul in his turn acknowledged the eminent standing of Peter, James, John and the other apostles (with whom James "the brother of the Lord" soon took a leading place). Those "Twelve" had been the first witnesses of Christ's resurrection, the foundation pillars of his Church, and the first preachers of the word. Paul describes how he had laid before them for approval an account of the gospel he preached to the Gentiles, "to make sure that the race I had run, and was running, should not be run in vain" (*Gal.* 2: 2). Yet on the other hand we can detect a separateness and independence in his attitude to them, with even a surprising note of irony in his references to "those reputed pillars" and "those superlative apostles" (*Gal.* 2 : 9; *2 Cor.* 11: 5). "I am a free man and own no master", he said boldly when comparing his apostolate with theirs (*1 Cor.* 9: 19). Fundamentally at one with them in faith and loyalty to Christ, and in his conviction of the indivisible unity of the Church in which Christ's Spirit dwelt, he could still criticize them, quarrel with them, and on occasion tell them "that their conduct did not square with the truth of the gospel". The Judaean brethren praised God for the fruits of Paul's preaching among the Gentiles, yet repeatedly we detect a reserve, at times even suspicion, in their attitude to him. His notoriety for disregard of the Jewish Law was a serious embarrassment to them (cf. *Acts* 21: 18–25). That this tension never developed into schism was perhaps due in no small measure to Paul's constant care to provide for the material necessities of "the saints" in Judaea from the resources of his congregations in Gentile lands.

I think that in Paul's own mind there was a kind of analogy between his relationship to the original apostles and the relationship of the Christian Church to the old Israel. The Israelites had been chosen and prepared for the Messianic destiny; yet in the event it was not the Jewish nation as such who proved to be the true elect and the true heirs of God's promises, but the unexpected offshoot from Israel—the Christian Church—with its large Gentile contingent. There was something similar in the way God had brought the gospel to the nations of mankind. Jesus had carefully chosen and prepared his own twelve apostles to preach his message and to carry on his saving work; to these apostles his resurrection was first revealed and they were the witnesses authorized to proclaim it. And yet in the event it was none of the twelve whom God's grace marked out to be the chief herald of the gospel to the Gentiles. Paul was humbly penitent when he recalled what he had been, but he was unhesitantly proud when he affirmed what God had made him. His own words explicitly invited his readers to see an analogy between, on the one hand, the free and disconcerting grace with which God had chosen for his favour the new believers rather than the old Israel, and, on the other, the free and disconcerting grace with which God had chosen Paul, an upstart and a late-comer in the Church, to be his apostle to the nations, rather than any of the original founding pillars of the Church:

"In the end he appeared even to me; though this birth of mine was monstrous, for I had persecuted the Church of God and am therefore inferior to all other apostles—indeed not fit to be called an apostle. However, by God's grace I am what I am, nor has his grace been given to me in vain; on the contrary, in my labours I have outdone them all—not I, indeed, but the grace of God working with me" (*1 Cor.* 15: 8–10; cf. *2 Cor.* 4: 1).

Of course the analogy I have indicated applied only in one respect: namely, that in both cases there was an unpredictable divine choice of an unexpected recipient of grace in the execution of God's plan. But in another important respect the analogy did *not* apply. Paul had no thought of pressing the analogy to the extent of implying that the original apostles and the Jewish-Christian trunk of the Church had rejected Christ's message, and that he himself and the newly engrafted growth of the Pauline churches had been chosen instead. In the passage just quoted he goes straight on to say: "But what matter, I or they? This [namely, the gospel of the risen Christ] is what we all proclaim, and this is what you believed."

Not altogether surprisingly, we find traces of a severely critical judgment on Paul in some Jewish-Christian circles in the generations after his death. In the Church at large, however, and in Rome in particular, he was ranked next to Peter in esteem. There can be no doubt of the formative influence of Paul's letters on the development of Christian doctrine. We get a hint of the authority they soon acquired in the letter which is known as *2 Peter*, which probably dates from the first quarter of the second century. The pseudonymous author referred to the wisdom with which Paul was endowed and ranked his letters with "the other Scriptures". This judgment was confirmed by the usage of other second-century Christian writers, for we find them too citing texts from Paul's letters as they would cite texts of the Old Testament.

CHAPTER III

ST. PAUL'S CONVERSION

by

Harold Wilson

ST. PAUL'S conversion lies at a point between eighteen months and five years after the death of Jesus, and his writings are earlier than the gospels. Paul came into the Christian movement when it was gradually finding its feet as a special form of piety within Judaism. He was dead before the final break with Judaism.

We have five accounts of the conversion of Paul and its attendant circumstances, supplemented by the apostle with his own religious experience, which is really of far more interest than the story itself.

Paul twice speaks of his having been converted from a persecutor into an ardent worshipper of Jesus, and two speeches describing the event are put into his mouth in *Acts*, Luke already having given an account of his own. We shall leave the important testimony in *Galatians* until later and first look at the narratives in *Acts*.

The conversion of Saul, the alleged instigator of the death of Stephen, is related dramatically in *Acts* 8 and 9. There is a lack of detail which we should gladly like to have in order to get an accurate idea of what actually happened. We are transported from one scene to another.

First, we witness the cruel death of the first martyr, Stephen, with the executioners casting their garments at the feet of a young man, Saul, who was consenting to Stephen's death. Unmoved, or rather excited to fury by this terrible spectacle, this man proceeds to further extremities, entering into the houses of believers in Jesus, arresting them and putting them in prison (*Acts* 7: 58; 8: 1–3 and 26: 9–11). Not content with what he had done in Jerusalem he obtained letters from the High Priest to the synagogues in Damascus authorizing him to arrest those he might find "of the way", and send them for trial in Jerusalem (*Acts* 9: 2).

Saul was accompanied by colleagues of this Jewish inquisition. As he came near to Damascus he was struck with a blinding light.

"Saul, Saul, why persecutest thou me?" He fell to the ground and was told to go to the city, "and there it shall be told you what you have to do". When arose he was completely blind. His companions did not understand; they left him in Damascus refusing to eat or drink. His abandonment by his companions as a sick man, unable to continue his mission, makes what follows more easily understood (*Acts 9*: 8–9).

Ananias—a disciple at Damascus—is then warned in a vision of the Lord Jesus to go to Saul's house (*Acts* 9: 10f). Ananias naturally remonstrates at a command to visit a known persecutor, but he is reassured (Acts 9: 10–19).

Saul to the astonishment of all appeared in the synagogue and confused the Jews in Damascus by proving that Jesus was the Son of God, the only time we find this expression in *Acts* (*Acts 9: 20–22*). They were provoked, and a plot was made to kill him, but he escaped by being lowered down the city wall in a basket (*Acts* 9: 25; *2 Cor.* 11: 33).

We next find Paul at Jerusalem where the disciples refused to receive him until Barnabas introduced him and related what had happened.

We note here that there were two groups—in Jerusalem Hebrew (Aramaic)-speaking Christians, in Damascus Greek-speaking Christians and Hellenistic Jews. Paul had been the leader of these Hellenistic Jews; he now became a missionary to them. They also turned on him and sought his life, but with the aid of the disciples he escaped to Caesarea and went home to Tarsus (*Acts* 9: 26–30).

The two speeches in which the conversion is related are in *Acts* 22, an address to the Sanhedrin in Jerusalem, and in *Acts* 26, his defence before Herod Agrippa II. The details differ but the facts are the same.

This brings us to the apostle's own account of the incident (*2 Cor.* 11: 32–33). He says nothing about a vision on his way to Damascus but he insists that he has seen the risen Lord Jesus. He does not mention Ananias (*Acts* 9 and 22) nor his baptism. He does write of his escape from Damascus (*2 Cor.* 11: 32). This gives the story a different complexion.

Finally there is the statement in *Galatians* 1: 13–21.

"For ye have heard of my conversation in time past in the Jews' religion, how that beyond measure I persecuted the church of God and wasted it; and profited in the Jews' religion above many my equals in mine own nation, being more exceedingly zealous of the traditions of my fathers. But when it pleased God, who separated me from my mother's womb, and called me by his grace, to reveal his Son in me, that I might preach him among the heathen: immediately I confessed not with flesh and blood: neither went I up to Jerusalem to them which were apostles before me; but I went into Arabia, and returned again unto Damascus. Then after three years I went up to Jerusalem to see Peter and abode with him fifteen days. But other of the apostles saw I none, save James the Lord's brother. Now the things which I write unto you, behold, before God I lie not. Afterwards I came into the regions of Syria and Cilicia."

This solemn testimony differs materially from the narrative in *Acts*. Nothing is said of Ananias nor of the preaching at Damascus immediately after the conversion. On the contrary Paul says that he withdrew to Arabia without consulting anyone. This is a much more probable story. The other story is suspicious, for example, entering the synagogue; nor is it likely that he would have gone to Jerusalem, where he was well known as a violent opponent of the cause he had now espoused.

It is not easy to say exactly what happened amidst so much conflicting testimony; all of it including Paul's own story is given many years after the event. It is only by conjecture that we can construct a connected story.

It looks as if *Acts* 9 appears to compress into a few verses events which extended over some time. Paul says that three years elapsed before his visit to Peter in Jerusalem. It is clear that Paul devoted his energies to the Hellenistic Jews rather than the Hebraic—he both persecuted and preached Jesus as a Greek-speaking Jew. We can infer that his dealings with the Jerusalem Christians were only occasional and slight. Damascus was at that time outside the frontiers of the Roman world and was a Greek-speaking city. In *Acts* 9: 29 Paul speaks to Hellenists in Jerusalem. In *Galatians* he implies that after his visit to Arabia his work was in Syria and Cilicia (*Gal.* 1: 21).

The real difficulty is what Paul relates to the Galatians about himself. Though he was unknown personally to the churches of Judaea in Christ, yet his fame as a preacher among the Gentiles had spread—"They were glorifying God in me". This went on for fourteen years, making seventeen since his conversion.

The writer of *Acts* tells us nothing of this long period, a period of very active missionary enterprise among the Gentiles. Even if we make allowance for the narrative of *Acts* being greatly compressed, it is difficult to reconcile it with statements in *Galatians* (*Acts* 9: 26–30; 11: 19–30). This account relates Paul's doings from his first visit to Jerusalem to the sending forth of the mission to Antioch.

Acts tells us that after being converted and preaching Christ in Damascus, he escaped and went to Jerusalem, where he tried to join the disciples. They did not believe him until Barnabas supported him. Paul disputed with Hellenistic Jews in Jerusalem and they tried to kill him. The brethren sent him to Caesarea and Tarsus. There is no hint as to how long he stayed, but a note which is appended may cover some considerable period. This shows us how little we really know of the progress of the Faith in the first twenty-five years after the Resurrection. It looks from the account as if Paul stayed in Tarsus until Barnabas fetched him and brought him to Antioch.

Acts is an attractive narrative but we must give good weight to Paul's own testimony. Both accounts are much later than the event. It is possible that Paul was carrying on a quiet missionary work all through these seventeen years. We hear only of his later successes. It is probable that he first preached to the Jews (*Acts* 9: 22) and to Hellenists (*Acts* 9: 29) and made no attempt to found Gentile churches till he reached Antioch in Pisidia (*Acts* 13: 14).

The facts of the vision near Damascus and the subsequent story fade into insignificance when we read the description of his own mental condition and the way in which he found peace and satisfaction in accepting Jesus Christ as his Master.

We can see his motivation in the epistle to the Romans.

He endeavours to show that the Law which Moses gave was good in every respect but a real trap for those who knew it. No mortal man had power to keep it in its entirety. It therefore did not save but only pointed out how far man had strayed from God. The Law was "Holy, just and good" but at the same time not life but death to the human race. The argument runs:

The law is spiritual, man is flesh and blood. I am therefore the slave of sin. I *desire* to do what is right, but I have no *power* to *perform* it. I am therefore in a wretched plight. "Who shall deliver me from this body which is nothing but death?" (*Rom.* 7: 24).

Answer: God delivered his servant from the state of misery by the Lord Jesus Christ who has destroyed sin in the believer in order that he is now able to serve God (*Rom.* 8: 1–14).

This account of the internal struggle is much later than his conversion. His conversion is not of a profligate to a life of virtue but of a very devoutly religious man to another point of view. He had not "given up" or had a nervous breakdown. He rarely refers to the acts and words of Jesus during his ministry. It was his devotion to Law which made him so bitter towards the new sect.

Two things may have converged together to cause his conversion:
1. Dissatisfaction with the power of the Law to make him conform to the will of God.
2. The realization that the future religion of the world would be either Pharisaic Judaism, or the new belief in Jesus.

To so ardent a spirit as Paul Jesus was either absolutely right or absolutely wrong; there was no middle way. The flood of light, hypnosis and blindness all point to signs of abnormality. It has been suggested that he suffered from epilepsy. So did Alfred the Great and Napoleon. Paul was an abnormal man; an ordinary man would not have achieved what he did.

CHAPTER IV

ST. PAUL THE MISSIONARY

by

Ivor Bulmer-Thomas

PART I: THE SOURCES

ST. PAUL was not the first Christian missionary in point of time: so far as the evidence is available, that title belongs to Philip the Deacon (*Acts* 8: 4–13, 26–40). Though his travels were the most extensive recorded in the New Testament, they were confined to a relatively small area around the Mediterranean, and have been far eclipsed in extent by later missionaries, notably St. Francis Xavier. But in the influence that he exerted, and in the permanence of his conquests for the Christian faith, St. Paul undoubtedly ranks first among all Christian missionaries. The most important moment in the long history of Europe was that when Paul saw in a vision a man of Macedonia saying, "Come over into Macedonia and help us" (*Acts* 16: 9).* Though Jewish Christians had already taken the message to Rome, it is from this moment that the Christianization of Europe with all its momentous consequences really begins.

And what a life of adventure Paul the Missionary led! It has remained unexcelled among all missionary activity. Let us recall his own words, forced from him to justify himself against "false apostles, deceitful workers, transforming themselves with the apostles of Christ" (*2 Cor.* 11: 13), more especially as we shall not be able to identify the precise time and location of all the trials that he relates.

"Are they ministers of Christ? (I speak as a fool) I am more; in labours more abundant, in stripes above measure, in prisons more frequent, in deaths oft. Of the Jews, five times received I forty stripes save one. Thrice was I beaten with rods, once was I stoned, thrice I suffered shipwreck, a night and a day I have been

---

* Unless there is reason for not so doing, scriptural quotations in this essay will be given in the familiar words of the Authorized Version; otherwise they will be directly translated.

in the deep; in journeyings often, in perils of waters, in perils of robbers, in perils by mine own countrymen, in perils by the heathen, in perils in the city, in perils in the wilderness, in perils in the sea, in perils among false brethren; in weariness and painfulness, in watchings often, in hunger and thirst, in fastings often, in cold and nakedness. Besides those things that are without, that which cometh upon me daily, the care of all the churches" (*2 Cor.* 11: 23–28).

To this memorable catalogue we may certainly add a further shipwreck on his journey as a captive to Rome, at least one and probably two periods of imprisonment in the capital, and finally the severance of his head from his body by the sword of a Roman executioner. It is not surprising that St. Paul is the archetypal missionary.

There are two main sources for St. Paul's missionary activities, his own letters and the *Acts of the Apostles* (more correctly, *Acts of Apostles*, as we shall see). The apocryphal *Acts of St. Paul* adds a few details which may be genuine, including his martyrdom to which reference has just been made, but by and large it is to St. Paul's *Epistles* and *Acts* that we must look for an account of his missionary work.

In neither of those sources can we expect a complete and systematic account of that work. The letters, with the notable exception of that to the Romans, were written as occasion demanded, to rebuke, to exhort, to justify, and as often as not were fired off in the heat of controversy. It is only occasionally that they throw light upon their author's life at a particular moment; but how precious that light is when it comes, we shall see.

Acts is more systematically written, and the second part is devoted entirely to Paul's doings, proceeding in chronological order. But even in the second part of *Acts* it would be wrong to expect a complete and detailed account of Paul's activities. *Acts* is certainly meant to be history, but like all historians the author writes from a standpoint, and like many historians he probably writes with a purpose. He is therefore selective in his material, choosing that which suits his standpoint and purpose. The historian is no mere annalist, cataloguing everything that happens, but from Thucydides onwards the historian has always carefully chosen his material so that his final product is as much a work of art as of science, being in fact neither a work of art nor of science but of history.

What are the main themes that emerge from a reading of *Acts*? One would appear to be to show St. Peter and St. Paul as the main figures in the building of the Christian Church. St. Peter dominates the first part of *Acts* almost as much as St. Paul dominates the second, and apart from the protomartyr St. Stephen and the deference paid to St. James, "the Lord's brother", in his special role as the local leader of the Church at Jerusalem hardly anyone else makes more than a shadowy appearance. This cannot be the whole truth. The other apostles could hardly have been entirely inactive, and it is more than probable that what tradition asserts about some of them—St. John in Asia Minor, St. Andrew in Scythia, St. Thomas in Parthia and India, for example—contains a kernel of fact. The correct title of the book, it should be emphasized, is not *The Acts of the Apostles* but *Acts of Apostles* [1] —that is, some acts of some apostles, and in particular of Peter and Paul. The author has deliberately concentrated the limelight on these two, and he began the process which ended with the acceptance by the Roman Church of these two as its joint founders, and their commemoration in a single feast on 29th June.

Here we come to a second chief purpose in *Acts*. The second part, as we have said, is devoted almost entirely to the activities of Paul, and a significant feature is that it ends with his arrival as a prisoner in Rome, awaiting trial. If the author had been aware at the time of writing that Paul had died by the executioner's sword, it is most improbable that he would not have ended with the martyrdom. It follows that *Acts* was written while Paul was a prisoner in Rome awaiting trial.[2]

---

[1] The title *Acta omnium apostolorum* in the Muratorian Canon shows what readers expected to find in it but in fact did not find.

[2] There is not a scrap of evidence to support the view that the author of *Acts* wrote, or intended to write, a sequel describing Paul's martyrdom. The theory put forward by W. M. Ramsay, *St. Paul the Traveller and the Roman Citizen*, pp. 27–28, that *ton men prōton logon* in *Acts* 1: 1 instead of *ton men proteron logon* implies that the Third Gospel and *Acts* were two parts of a trilogy was doubtful in his own day and no longer convinces. As Ernst Haehnchen, *The Acts of the Apostles*, p. 137, n. 1, observes: "Luke Hellenistically employs *prōron* and *prōtos* for *proteros* without implying that there was a *tritos*". The hypothesis here put forward, implying that *Acts* must have been written by A.D. 64, and therefore the second and third gospels earlier still, though not necessarily in their present forms, will startle many modern scholars, wedded to the theory of a late date for *Acts*, but it is the duty of scholars to follow wherever the argument leads, however inconvenient it may be. This dating for *Acts* has at least the support of one scholar whom no one could call conservative—A. Harnack, *Beiträge* IV, 81, *Neue Untersuchungen zur Apostelgeschichte und zur Abfassungszeit der synoptischen Evangelien*, Eng. trans., *The Date of Acts and of the Synoptic Gospels* (London, 1911). It is strongly corroborated by the fact that the author shows no awareness of any of St. Paul's letters, although by the time 2 *Peter* was written these had already acquired the status of Holy Writ (2 *Peter* 3: 15–16). (See below, p. 61.)

Acts, then, is selective as well as the epistles, and the selection is different. It is necessary to make this point as some modern scholars pin their faith to one or the other but not both. In a much acclaimed recent work, for example, Günther Bornkamm maintains, "Paul's letters are the primary and normative source not only for his message and theology, but also for the first subject to be discussed in this book, his life",[3] and he dismisses *Acts* as a compilation of little historical value written "more than forty years after Paul's letters".[4] The argument is unconvincing. One reason given is the alleged discrepancy between the letters and *Acts*, but all these disappear when they are closely examined. It would take us far outside the bounds of this essay to examine them all in detail, but we may take one, which is relevant to our purpose, as an example. In his letters Paul frequently lays claim to the title of apostle. They begin, "Paul . . . called *to be* an apostle" (*Rom.* 1: 1), "Paul, called *to be* an apostle" (*1 Cor.* 1: 1), "Paul an apostle of Jesus Christ" (*2 Cor.* 1: 1) and so on; while in *1 Cor.* 9: 1 he indignantly asks, "Am I not an apostle? Have I not seen Jesus Christ our Lord?" In *Acts* the title apostle is never directly given to Paul as a title, though in two places it is given to him along with Barnabas implicitly (14: 4, 14). It would appear that according to the prevailing school of thought in the early Church the term apostle was reserved for those who had been our Lord's chief companions in his earthly life, and that the author of *Acts*, despite his tremendous admiration for Paul, probably shared this point of view. But Paul himself regarded his vision of Christ on the road to Damascus as qualifying him for the title ("Have I not seen Jesus Christ our Lord?") and had no hesitation in claiming it. The question arises whether Paul was ever fully accepted in the original apostolic circle. We know from the middle chapters of *Acts* the hesitations that were felt. That the Church in due course placed him on an equality with Peter and the other apostles may in large part be due to the sympathetic and convincing portrayal of his life and work in *Acts*.

If a choice had to be made between the epistles and *Acts* as a historical source, it is not at all evident that the former should be chosen. No contemporary biographer writing the life of, say, Winston Churchill or Lloyd George, would accept without question what they had to say about themselves. Though this must be taken into consideration, and may be the best or only source for particular events, their knowledge of certain situations may

[3] *Paul*, p. xiv.
[4] *Ibid.*, p. xv.

have been partial, their memory may have played tricks with them,[5] or they may have been deliberately trying to cut a figure on the stage of history. The biographer will not be satisfied that he has the correct picture until he has "worked over the papers" as historians say.

So it is with *Acts*. The author has "worked over the papers", metaphorically if not literally. This raises the question who that author was. It is not possible here to go into that question in detail, but the identification of the author both of the third gospel and of *Acts* with St. Luke, a Gentile and "the beloved physician" of *Col.* 4: 14 (*cf. Col.* 4: 11), is highly probable on internal grounds and has never been convincingly challenged. In certain passages of *Acts* (the "we passages", *Acts* 16: 10–17, 20: 5 – 21: 18, 27: 1 – 28: 16) the author writes as though he was Paul's travelling companion at those times, and the simplest explanation is that he was.[6] In certain passages of Paul's letters (*Col.* 2: 14, *2 Tim.* 4: 11 [7]) it is implied that Luke was with Paul during his captivity in Rome. If those assumptions are correct—and there seems no reason to doubt them—he wrote from personal experience about some of the events he describes and he had ample opportunity to learn about the others from the lips of Paul himself and his companions.

If this argument is valid, there is every reason to treat *Acts* with respect as a historical source, and if it were a secular work it would undoubtedly be regarded by secular scholars as a primary source for the political, legal, social and religious life of the eastern half of the Mediterranean in the first century of the Christian era. But more important than this balance of probabilities is the fact that *Acts* has been triumphantly vindicated as a source at every point where it has proved possible to test it. A big step in establishing the authenticity of *Acts* was taken by that great scholar, William Mitchell Ramsay (Sir William Ramsay) in a series of books at the end of the nineteenth and beginning of the twentieth century, and they can still be read with advantage. The most important single confirmation of the narrative in *Acts* took place in

---

[5] I recall a fierce altercation in the House of Commons between Ernest Bevin and Winston Churchill on the subject of a Cabinet decision about the atomic bomb: when the Cabinet minute was studied the memory of both was proved to be at fault.

[6] The theory put forward by M. Dibelius and endorsed by G. Bornkamm (*Paul*, p. xx) that the author made use of an "itinerary" or "travel diary", omitting to alter the first person plural in it, is implausible.

[7] St. Paul's authorship of *2 Tim.* is disputed (see below), but the statement about Luke could still be true even if he were not the author.

1894, when four fragments of an inscription found at Delphi [8] established that Lucius Junius Gallio,[9] brother of the philosopher Seneca, was proconsul of Achaia, just as St. Luke said he was (*Acts* 18: 12): and this gives us a fixed point in the Pauline chronology, for the inscription shows that Gallio's year as proconsul ran either from 1st May 51 to 1st May 52 or from 1st May 52 to 1st May 53, with the balance of probability in favour of Gallio's arrival on 1st May 51.[10] It is implied that the Jews made their complaints to the new proconsul as soon as possible after his arrival, and Paul would have left Corinth in the summer of 51; as he had stayed there for eighteen months (*Acts* 18: 11), he would have arrived in Corinth in the winter of 49–50. When he arrived there he found Aquila and Priscilla, who had recently arrived (*Acts* 18: 2) on account of an expulsion of Jews from Rome by the Emperor Claudius.[11] This expulsion is dated by Orosius to 49, and therefore there is complete harmony in the sources.

It would be unreasonable to expect such detailed proof—or disproof—of every statement made by Luke in *Acts;* this will depend upon the fruits of excavations or other discoveries yet to be made. But a classical historian of undoubted competence and integrity, Mr. A. N. Sherwin-White, has recently published a book, *Roman Society and Roman Law in the New Testament,* which trenchantly vindicates the Lucan narrative at a large number of points. In such matters as Roman legal processes and the

---

[8] Dittenberger, *Sylloge Inscriptionum Graecarum*, 3rd ed., II 801 D. For a discussion of the inscription see F. J. Foakes-Jackson and Kirsopp Lake (eds.), *The Beginnings of Christianity*, Vol. V, pp. 460–464, or C. K. Barrett, *The New Testament Background: Selected Documents*, p. 48.

[9] His proper name was Marcus Annaeus Novatus, but he took the name of the wealthy Lucius Junius Gallio who adopted him. He was the son of the Spanish orator and financier Marcus Annaeus Seneca, and was the elder brother of the philosopher Seneca, who dedicated the *De ira* and *De vita beata* to him. Like his brother he was forced to commit suicide by Nero.

[10] The detailed argument is too long to give here but may be followed in Ernst Haenchen, *The Acts of the Apostles*, p. 66 and notes.

[11] Suetonius says that the expulsion was on account of continual disturbances caused by Chrestus (*Iudaeos impulsore Chresto assidue tumultuantis Roma expulit,* Suetonius, *De vita Caesarum* V, "Divus Claudius", 25. 4). Almost certainly Chrestus is here to be interpreted as the leader of the *Chrestiani* or *Christiani,* that is, Christ, assumed through ignorance to be actually living at the time. Dion Cassius relates that it was found so difficult to keep the Jews out of Rome on account of their numbers that the Emperor did not in fact expel them but made stricter regulations for their behaviour. No doubt, however, an attempt to expel them was made, and some would have obeyed, including Aquila and Priscilla.

rights attaching to Roman citizenship it is established on the basis of a far-ranging knowledge of ancient texts that St. Luke was meticulously accurate. In particular, what St. Luke alleges to have happened is shown to be in accordance with the practice of the middle of the first century but it would frequently not be in accordance with the practice of the end of the first century or of the second century. After Sherwin-White's critical dissection there need be no further hesitation in accepting the account of Paul's travels in *Acts* as being substantially trustworthy.

One further point needs to be made. In the hundreds of New Testament manuscripts there are many variant readings in all the books, but in the case of *Acts* one of the texts, embodied in Codex Bezae, commonly designated D and located at Cambridge, differs so markedly from the other manuscripts that it needs to be specially considered.[12] This "Western text" has the appearance of being a revision of an earlier text, and if we are right in saying that Luke wrote *Acts* during Paul's first imprisonment it is possible that he had still enough life before him to make the revision himself. At any rate many of the readings in D are inherently plausible, and are to be preferred over the other manuscripts. As an example, if D is followed in *Acts* 11: 28, Luke was one of the first members of the Christian community at Antioch, which would help to account for his interest in, and special information about, the church in that city. It is just the sort of addition that Luke might have made in writing a second edition—or someone revising the text after his death.

The upshot of this somewhat long but necessary preliminary discussion of sources is that both the letters and *Acts* may be accepted as authentic sources for St. Paul's missionary activity. Let us now see what these sources indicate.

PART II: ST. PAUL'S TRAVELS

Even at this point we cannot go straight to St. Paul's three well-documented missionary journeys. There is a long period after his conversion—at least fourteen years—of which we know practically nothing. From his own account (*Gal.* 1: 17) we know that after his conversion he went into Arabia, that is, *Arabia Petraea*, then

---

[12] A. C. Clark, *The Acts of the Apostles* (Oxford, 1933) gives pre-eminence to the readings in D.

the vassal kingdom of the Nabataeans adjoining Damascus, and although this territory at that time is not to be regarded as a desert it is more than probable that St. Paul there sought solitude in order to meditate and re-orient himself after his traumatic experience. From these meditations he returned to Damascus, and after three years (*Gal.* 1: 18) he went to Jerusalem to question Peter and spent a fortnight with him. (The primacy of Peter among the Apostles is here recognized and we have a foretaste of the "pairing" of SS. Peter and Paul by the later Roman church.) From *Acts* 9: 26–28 we know that on this visit he tried to join himself to the disciples, but they were all afraid of him and doubted the genuineness of his conversion. The great-hearted Barnabas then took him and brought him "to the apostles"—probably a "rhetorical plural" meaning simply the Christian leaders in Jerusalem as Paul himself says roundly that of the other apostles besides Peter he saw none save James, the Lord's brother (*Gal.* 1: 19). He would naturally see James, who appears to have held a local primacy in Jerusalem, taking precedence there even over Peter. Paul then seems to have been accepted by the Christian community there, "with them coming in and going out at Jerusalem".

On leaving Jerusalem he went into the regions of Syria and Cilicia (1: 21) and "was unknown by face unto the churches of Judaea which were in Christ" (1: 22). After an uncertain number of years Barnabas went from Antioch to St. Paul's native city, Tarsus in Cilicia, to enlist his aid in the great city on the Orontes (*Acts* 11: 25–26), after Rome and Alexandria the third city of the Roman empire.

What was he doing in Syria and Cilicia in the meantime? It is sometimes conjectured[13] that he was already engaged in missionary work. This may be so, and it will be recalled how immediately after his conversion "straightway he preached Christ in the synagogues" (*Acts* 9: 20). But we also know that the Christians found it difficult to accept their former persecutor (*Acts* 9: 21), and it may be that throughout this Syrian and Cilician period he was still seeking to adjust himself to his new beliefs. We may compare another famous convert, John Henry Newman. From his conversion to the Roman Catholic Church in 1845 to 1864 his life was one of frustration and disappointment. It was not until Charles Kingsley's accusation of dishonesty wrung from him his *Apologia* that he gained self-confidence and entered a period of influence in his new communion. The length of time, fifteen years,

---

[13] By G. Bornkamm, *Paul*, pp. 26–29, it is asserted as a fact.

is almost the same as the great gap in Paul's life.[14] It was only when Barnabas deliberately sought him out to be a colleague that his great work began.

For a year after Barnabas had rescued him Paul taught at Antioch (*Acts* 11: 26). It was at this time and at Antioch that the disciples were first called Christians, a mocking term which they accepted proudly, as the British Expeditionary Force of 1914 gloried in the term "Old Contemptibles", or the politicians of an earlier century "Whigs" and "Tories". Then a famine arose,[15] and the Christian community at Antioch decided to send alms to the Christians of Jerusalem—it is the beginning of "Peter's Pence" —and chose Barnabas and Paul for the purpose (*Acts* 11: 29).

With a high degree of probability this visit—St. Paul's second visit to Jerusalem—is to be identified with that which he describes in *Gal.* 2: 1-10. It is often supposed that the visit mentioned in *Galatians* is to be identified with the Council of Jerusalem described in *Acts* 15, but, even allowing for differences of viewpoint, the visit mentioned by Paul is hardly recognizable as the visit described by Luke. No difficulties arise if we accept that the visit described in *Galatians* took place before the Council of Jerusalem and is to be identified with the visit of *Acts* 11: 29–30 for the purpose of conveying alms. The visit described in *Galatians* ends with James, Peter and John, "who seemed to be pillars" (*Gal.* 2: 9) giving to Paul and Barnabas the right hand of fellowship and endorsing their work, but asking only that they should remember the poor (*Acts* 2: 10)—in other words, to carry on doing what they had come to do.[16]

The confusion with the Council of Jerusalem has arisen because the question of taking Christianity to the Gentiles was the main issue in both visits. This is not surprising. As soon as the disciples moved out of Judaea it was bound to arise. Those who were scattered on the death of Stephen went as far as Phoenicia and Cyprus and Antioch, we are told (*Acts* 11: 19), at first "preaching the word to none but the Jews only". But some men of Cyprus and Cyrene, when they came to Antioch, proclaimed the Lord Jesus to

---

[14] There is even a parallel to St. Paul's preaching in the synagogues immediately after his conversion in Newman's mission to Leeds, where his friend Pusey had just founded St. Saviour's Church.

[15] We need not press the words "great dearth throughout all the world, which came to pass in the days of Claudius Caesar" (*Acts* 11: 28) and try to identify it with a general famine, of which there is no evidence, in Claudius' reign.

[16] This view was cogently argued by W. M. Ramsay, *St. Paul the Traveller and Roman Citizen*, pp. 56–62.

"the Greeks".[17] The question whether Gentiles could be Christians was therefore already demanding answer when Paul arrived in Antioch, and his own answer could not be in doubt, for it had been the central theme of the speech by St. Stephen that provoked the Jews to the murderous assault in which he, Paul, had played a leading part, a part that troubled his conscience ever afterwards. The ostensible purpose of his visit was to convey alms, but, of course, he took the opportunity of discussing this central issue with James, Peter and John. He took Titus with him—Titus, who played a big part in Paul's life but for whom Luke could surprisingly find no place in his narrative in *Acts*[18]—and although Titus was a Greek he was not required to be circumcised. James, Peter and John agreed on that occasion that, while their mission was to "the circumcision", that is, to the Jews, it was right for Barnabas and Paul to preach Christ to the Gentiles: but the question was not finally settled. Peter, who had been taught in a vision not to call anything unclean which God had cleansed (*Acts* 10: 15) and had begun to eat with Gentiles, later under pressure ceased to do so, and even Barnabas followed his example. When Peter paid a visit to Antioch, Paul "withstood him to the face" (*Gal.* 2: 11). His argument was trenchant, but even so the issue was not resolved till the Council of Jerusalem.

Quite a long time had passed since Paul's conversion. According to his own account, three years had elapsed when he paid his first visit to Jerusalem and fourteen years when he paid his second visit. (Some would say seventeen years, by adding the periods together, but this is to create unnecessary difficulties for a possible, and perhaps the natural, meaning of "fourteen years after" in *Gal.* 2: 1 is "fourteen years after my conversion", the big event of his life.) If Christ was crucified in AD 30, St. Stephen may have been martyred in 33 and the second visit to Jerusalem and the return to Antioch may have taken place in 47, with a margin of a year or two either way.

We have reached a climax in Paul's life. In Luke's narrative *Acts* 13: 1–2 opens a new chapter in the metaphorical as well as

---

[17] This is the correct reading rather than "to the Hellenists", that is, Greek-speaking Jews as in *Acts* 6: 1. But even if "to the Hellenists" were correct, it could only be a matter of a short time before the question of preaching to the Gentiles would arise.

[18] W. M. Ramsay daringly suggests as the reason for the omission that Titus was a relative of Luke (*St. Paul the Traveller and Roman Citizen*, p. 390). Perhaps Luke did not think highly of Titus for one reason or another.

the literal sense. It is clearly meant to indicate a new departure. Let us have it in Luke's own words:

"Now there were in the church that was at Antioch certain prophets and teachers; as Barnabas, and Simeon that was called Niger, and Lucius of Cyrene, and Manaen, who had been brought up with Herod the tetrarch, and Saul.

"As they ministered to the Lord, and fasted, the Holy Ghost said, Separate me Barnabas and Saul for the work whereunto I have called them.

"And when they had fasted and prayed, and laid their hands on them, they sent them away."

It is the beginning of Paul's missionary activity in earnest, an activity that was to cease only with his death. His three missionary journeys and voyage to Rome were once, along with the kings of Israel, the main element in the religious knowledge of an educated Englishman, and although we can no longer make this assumption it will be sufficient to set them out in tabular form with approximate dates as follows:

First Journey 47–49

(Syrian) Antioch, Cyprus, Pamphylia, Pisidian Antioch, Iconium, Lystra, Derbe, Lystra, Iconium, Pisidian Antioch, Perga, Attalia, (Syrian) Antioch

[Council of Jerusalem 50]

Second Journey 50–52

(Syrian) Antioch, Galatia, Troas, Philippi, Thessalonica, Beroea, Athens, Corinth, Cenchreae, Ephesus, Caesarea, Jerusalem, (Syrian) Antioch

Third Journey 53–57

(Syrian) Antioch, Galatia, Phrygia, Ephesus, Macedonia, Achaia, Macedonia, Philippi, Troas, Assos, Mytilene, Chios, Samos (Trogyllium), Miletus, Coos, Rhodes, Patara, Tyre, Ptolemais, Caesarea, Jerusalem

[Imprisonment in Palestine 57–59]

Journey to Rome 59–60
Caesarea, Sidon, Myra, Fair Havens (Crete), "up and down in Adria", Melita, Syracuse, Rhegium, Puteoli, Forum of Appius, Three Taverns, Rome

[Imprisonment in Rome 60–62][19]

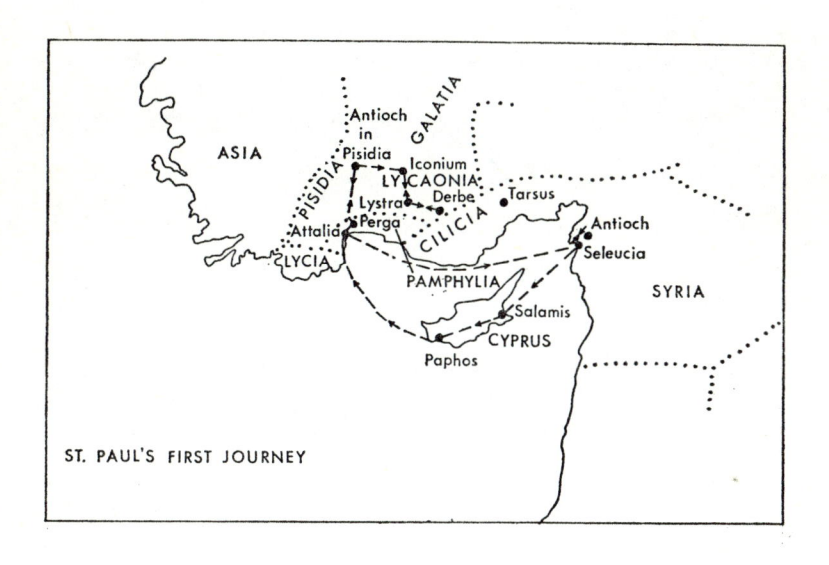

ST. PAUL'S FIRST JOURNEY

[19] The dates of Paul's third journey, his imprisonment in Palestine and his imprisonment in Rome could all possibly be placed up to two years later, putting his acquittal in AD 64, but hardly any later as he would certainly have perished in the Neronian persecution of that year if not released earlier. G. Bornkamm (*Paul*, p. xii) would have him imprisoned in Rome 58–60 and martyred in the latter year.

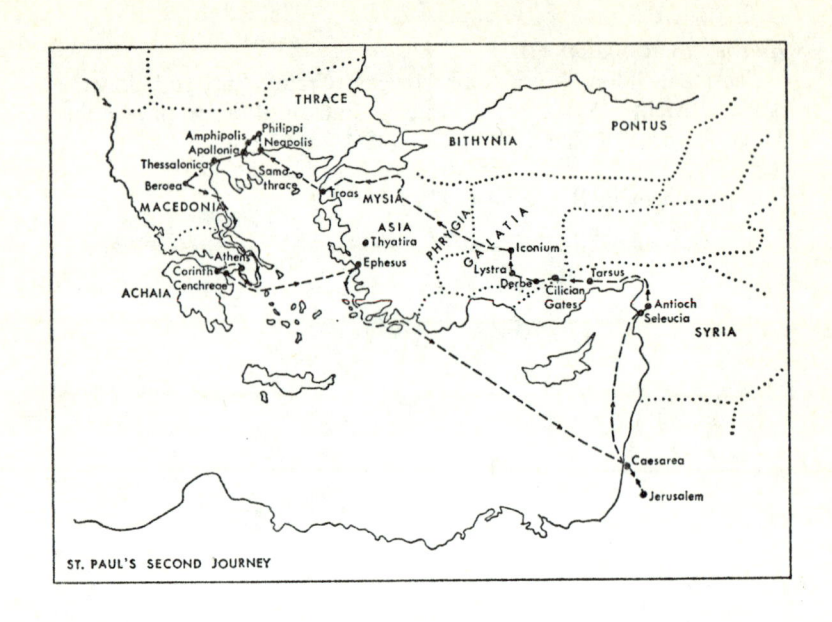

ST. PAUL'S SECOND JOURNEY

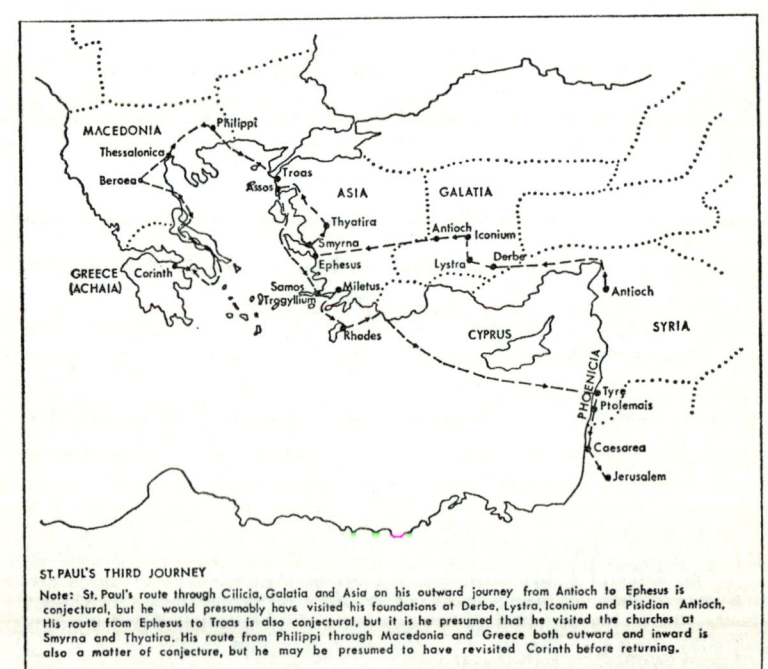

ST. PAUL'S THIRD JOURNEY

Note: St. Paul's route through Cilicia, Galatia and Asia on his outward journey from Antioch to Ephesus is conjectural, but he would presumably have visited his foundations at Derbe, Lystra, Iconium and Pisidian Antioch. His route from Ephesus to Troas is also conjectural, but it is he presumed that he visited the churches at Smyrna and Thyatira. His route from Philippi through Macedonia and Greece both outward and inward is also a matter of conjecture, but he may be presumed to have revisited Corinth before returning.

No attempt will here be made to describe these journeys in detail, as is done in several excellent publications, or to vindicate all the dates offered, and only a few general considerations will here be raised.

Firstly, how did Paul travel? We have few indications. Much of his journeying was by water. There were no passenger ships in those days,[20] and when he had a sea to cross he would wait until a ship with freight was going his way and pay the captain or owner for his passage. As for his land journeys, we are told that he went on foot from Troas to Assos on his third journey, but this was his deliberate choice while his companions went by sea; probably he wished to be alone to concentrate his thoughts. No doubt much of his journeying was done on foot, but he may have used a horse when one was available. (We know that he rode to Damascus on horseback before his conversion, and he was sent by Claudius Lysias from Jerusalem to Caesarea on horseback, *Acts* 23: 23-33, but then he had no choice.) There is no reason to doubt that on his missionary journeys Paul "roughed it". This is implied in his recollection, already mentioned, "in journeyings often, in perils of waters, in perils of robbers".

How did he support himself during his journeys and pay for such things as he had to pay for, including travelling expenses, books and writing materials for his many letters, and the use of the school of Tyrannus daily for two years at Corinth (*Acts* 19: 9-10)? No doubt he was not above accepting hospitality from his friends when it was offered. We know that Lydia, the well-to-do seller of purple whom he converted at Philippi, opened her house to him (*Acts* 16: 14-15, 40). We know that at Corinth he stayed with Aquila and Priscilla (*Acts* 18: 2), before settling with Justus hard by the synagogue, and the reason throws light on another feature of his missionary work. He was a worker-priest—or in his case perhaps we should say worker-bishop. Like Aquila and Priscilla he was a tent-maker.[21] This does not mean that he was a member of a guild, as a man who has never carved a joint might say that he was a butcher; he could and did make tents with his own hands, and by this trade he supported himself. As Haenchen

---

[20] The statement in *Acts* 27: 37 that there were 276 persons on board the ship which carried Paul towards Italy, if correct, would suggest a big passenger ship, but almost certainly this is a textual error; Codex Vaticanus and the Sahidic version give more credibly 76. (But Josephus says the ship in which he suffered shipwreck also on the way to Rome, had about 600 persons on board—*Vita* 15.)

[21] The traditional rendering is better than Haenchen's "leatherworker", for which I can think of no foundation.

conjectures, it was probably because he inquired where there was a master in his craft with whom he could work that he "found" Aquila[22]; and we are specifically told that they worked together. The fact that he was a highly-educated man from the university city of Tarsus who had sat at the feet of Gamaliel in Jerusalem did not in the least make him ashamed to work with his own hands. He was proud of his economic independence. While courteously thanking the church at Philippi for sending him gifts when a prisoner at Rome, he told them that he had learnt in whatever state he was therewith to be content, and he knew both how to be abased and how to abound (*Phil.* 4: 11–12). He was glad that he had not put the church at Corinth to expense in the past, and he would not do so in the future (*2 Cor.* 12: 13–18). At Miletus he told the elders whom he had summoned from Ephesus to hear a farewell address that he had coveted no man's silver or gold or apparel and added, "Yea, ye yourselves know, that these hands have ministered to my necessities, and to them that were with me" (*Acts* 20: 34).

Paul did not merely not depend on the Mother Church for his sustenance as a missionary but he made the collection of money for the Mother Church a main feature of his missionary work. He directed the church at Corinth, as he had previously directed the Galatian Christians, to set something by each Sunday according to their means—surely the first example of Christian stewardship—so that there would be no need to pass the plate round when he came, and they could nominate whom they wished to take their gifts to Jerusalem, including himself if they so desired (*1 Cor.* 16: 1–4). In two whole chapters of a later letter (*2 Cor.* 8–9) he stirred up the Corinthians by the example of the Macedonians, and by every argument of which he could think, to be liberal in their giving for "the ministering to the saints"; and he similarly stirred the Macedonians by the example of Achaia. He told the church in Rome how it had pleased the Christians of Macedonia and Achaia to make a collection for the poor saints at Jerusalem (*Rom.* 15: 26), and in his defence before Felix he stated that on his last journey to the Jewish capital he had come to bring alms to his nation, and offerings (*Acts* 24: 17). Those modern priests who complain that they ought to be freed from the burden of

---

[22] *The Acts of the Apostles*, p. 534. But Haenchen's further suggestion that he could carry on mission work in the synagogue only on the sabbath because he was earning his bread on work-days seems wide of the mark; other people had to earn their bread also, and it would be only on the sabbath that he would find substantial numbers there.

raising money might do well to consider the attention that Paul gave to it: and like him they might find it an instrument of evangelization.

How did Paul divide his time in his missionary work? On a cursory reading Luke's narrative gives the impression of constant movement, but a closer study shows that Paul spent long periods in the same place. He dug deep and sent down roots. His longest stay in one place was at Ephesus, where he spent at least two years and three months during his third journey after a preliminary reconnaissance on his second journey, a visit cut short by the need to get to Jerusalem for the Passover. It is highly probable that Ephesus, the capital of the Roman province of Asia, and the starting point of the great Roman road to the east, was made the centre for a mission to the whole of that province. Even if Luke may have been guilty of pardonable exaggeration when he wrote, "All they that dwelt in Asia heard the word of the Lord Jesus, both Jews and Greeks" (*Acts* 19: 10), it is more than likely that all "the seven churches which are in Asia" addressed in the Apocalypse (*Rev.* 1: 11) were founded at this time. Ephesus itself is the first named, and the others are Smyrna, Pergamos, Thyatira (of which Lydia was a native), Sardis, Philadelphia and Laodicea. Paul himself may not have been the founder of any of these churches, perhaps not even of Ephesus,[23] for there is no evidence or tradition to that effect; but by this time he had a body of devoted and able disciples, and he directed their activities. The church at

---

[23] On his first visit to Ephesus Paul merely reasoned with the Jews in the synagogue (*Acts* 18: 19) and then departed for the Passover feast in Jerusalem; and before he returned Apollos "spake and taught diligently the things of the Lord", but "knowing only the baptism of John" (*Acts* 18: 25). When Paul returned he found a band of twelve professing Christians who had been baptized "unto John's baptism" and knew not the Holy Ghost (*Acts* 19: 1–7). Aquila and Priscilla, whom Paul had left at Ephesus, instructed Apollos more perfectly, and Paul his disciples, and it can be argued whether Apollos, or Aquila and Priscilla, or Paul should be regarded as the founder of the Ephesian church.

The position of John the son of Zebedee also requires consideration. The tradition is strong that, as bidden from the cross by Jesus, he took care of the Blessed Virgin Mary and that she shared his home at Ephesus. When? There is no hint in *Acts* or in Paul's letters that John had been there before him. Even if Mary was only seventeen, as may well have been the case, when she gave birth to Jesus some time before 4 BC, she would have been a woman of at least seventy-five when Paul bade farewell to the Ephesian elders. As the last mention of Mary in the New Testament is her presence with the Apostles in an upper room at Jerusalem between the Ascension and Pentecost (*Acts* 1: 14), it is probable that her lodging with John was in Jerusalem, that she died early there, and that John's residence in Ephesus took place after Paul's arrest in Jerusalem and probably after his death.

Colossae, which was near to Laodicea, was certainly founded at this time, and probably by Paul's disciple Timothy; for when Paul came to write to the Colossians, Timothy is conjoined with him in the salutation (*Col.* 1: 1), and he added, "We give thanks to God and the Father of our Lord Jesus Christ, praying always for you, since we have heard of your faith in Christ Jesus" (*Col.* 1: 3–4), where the significance of the term "heard" must not be overlooked. The church in Laodicea, not yet become lukewarm as it had by the end of the century (*Rev.* 3: 15–16), is affectionately greeted in the same letter, and so is the church at Hierapolis, which need not necessarily have disappeared before the Apocalypse was written as the author needed the mystic number seven for his purpose. Both Onesimus and Epaphras are recorded as natives of Colossae (*Col.* 4: 9, 12).

Paul's stay in Corinth was also lengthy, at least eighteen months (*Acts* 18: 11). It was equally successful, the Lord saying to Paul in a vision, "I have much people in this city" (*Acts* 18: 10). Though there are fewer indications of time at other places, and his stay was probably a matter of months rather than of years, Paul always seems to have allowed himself time to settle down, and take stock of the situation, before beginning the attempt at conversion. He was not like some of the international evangelists of our own days who have the ground carefully prepared for them by a national committee before they step on the stage to a fanfare of trumpets and the switching on of the arc lamps.

What has just been said points to two of the main characteristics of Paul's missionary activity.

(a) He concentrated on the strategic points of the Roman Empire. As Roland Allen has written,[24] "St. Paul's theory of evangelizing

---

[24] *Missionary Methods*, 2nd ed. (London, 1968), pp. 12–13. This is a thoughtful study of Paul's missionary methods and their relevance in modern conditions. Allen asks, and attempts to answer, the following questions: "(1) How far was St. Paul's success due to the position or character of the places in which he preached? (2) Was his success due to the existence of a special class of people to which he made a special appeal? (3) Was the moral, social or religious condition of the provinces so unlike anything known in modern times as to render comparison between St. Paul's work and our own futile? (4) How far was St. Paul's success due to his possession of miraculous powers? (5) How far was his success due to his financial arrangements? (6) How far was his success due to his method of preaching? (7) How far was St. Paul's success due to the teaching which he gave to his converts? (8) How far was his success due to his method of preparing his candidates for baptism and ordination? (9) How far was St. Paul's success due to his manner of exercising authority and discipline? (10) How did he succeed in maintaining unity?"

a province was not to preach in every place in it himself, but to establish centres of Christian life in two or three important places from which the knowledge might spread into the country round. ... All the cities, or towns, in which he planted churches were centres of Roman administration, of Greek civilization, of Jewish influence, or of some commercial importance." His base was Antioch, already becoming so influential that a Roman poet was soon to complain that the Orontes had flowed with the Tiber. His first conquest was in the capital of Cyprus, and the places of his subsequent activity—Iconium, Philippi, Thessalonica, Beroea, Athens, Corinth, Ephesus—were nearly all centres of influence until he reached the capital itself, eternal Rome. Like the Jesuits of the sixteenth and seventeenth centuries he directed his efforts at the centres of power, they to the temporal rulers, he to the centres of political and commercial power, and not infrequently to the rulers therein.

(b) He was not merely an individualist, though he could be as individual as anyone when the occasion demanded, but was the leader of a team. He gathered round himself a band of able men and women whose activities he directed. He took great care in their training for baptism and ordination, and when they had proved their loyalty and worth he delegated great responsibility to them. This feature of his work is bound up with the other just mentioned, for while Paul directed operations from the strategic headquarters they carried the assault into the surrounding country. He was rewarded for his trust by their almost complete self-effacement. Their names are nevertheless written, not only in the Book of Life, but in the salutations of Paul's own letters—Timothy and Titus, Silas (= Sylvanus), Luke, Aquila and Priscilla, Apollos, Mark, Epaphras, clearly in the front rank, and among the lesser figures Clement (was he the author of the sub-apostolic letter to the Corinthians and an early bishop of Rome?), Linus (also an early bishop of Rome?), Sosthenes (was he the same person as the head of the Corinthian synagogue beaten in front of Gallio by the enraged Jews and converted by Paul as Crispus had been before him?), Stephanas, Fortunatus and Achaicus, Phoebe, Epaenetus, "the first-fruits of Achaia unto Christ" (*Rom.* 16: 5), Mary of Rome, Andronicus and Junia, Amplias, Urbane and Stachys, Apelles, his kinsman Herodion, Tryphena and Tryphosa, Persis, Rufus, Asyncritus, Phlegon, Hermas, Patrobas, Hermes, Philologus and Julia, Nereus and his sister, Olympas, Lucius and Jason, his kinsman Sosipater, Tertius one of his amanuenses, Gaius, Erastus and Quartus, Philemon, Euodias and Syntyche, Tychicus,

Onesimus, Jesus Justus, Demas, Nymphas, Archippus, Trophimus, Eubulus, Pudens, Claudia, Zenas the lawyer (was he engaged for Paul's defence?). The number of names—and there is no reason to suppose we know them all—indicates a formidable team, and there is nothing like it among the other early Christian leaders. In human terms, Paul could not have accomplished all that he did but for them. Incidentally, the number of female names in the list shows that Paul was no misogynist. In his remarks about women and their apparel he was merely echoing the conventions of his day.

What was Paul's method in his missions? His universal rule was, "To the Jew first, and also to the Gentile" (*Rom.* 2: 10). Though convinced from the time of his conversion that Christianity must be a universal religion, in which there is "neither Jew nor Greek . . . neither bond nor free . . . neither male nor female" (*Gal.* 3: 28), he was punctilious in deferring to the sensibilities of his fellow-Jews, and whenever there was a local congregation he always began his work by speaking there. It would be the normal practice for a stranger like himself attending synagogue worship to be asked by the leader of the synagogue after the reading of the law and the prophets if he had any message for the people. This attendance at Jewish worship had, of course, practical advantages for he had in the synagogue a ready-made church building and in the congregation a captive audience. The idea that the early Christians had no churches is a misunderstanding of what actually happened until Christianity was forced underground. As F. H. Chase has written,[25] "Christianity, absolutely new in its central ideas and aims, employed time-honoured machinery for their furtherance. . . . A special instance of this general characteristic of Christianity is found in the relation of the Church to the Synagogue. To the Synagogue system, speaking from a human point of view, the Church owes it that she outlived the days of her immaturity and weakness. Here was an organization ready to hand, which she could use and gradually mould after her own higher type of life. Here was a network encircling within its meshes the whole Roman Empire by which the Church could draw Gentile as well as Jew to herself."

The pattern of Paul's missionary work was set on his first journey at Pisidian Antioch. There he and Barnabas went into the synagogue on the sabbath, and after the reading of the law

---

[25] Frederic Henry Chase, *Texts and Studies*, Vol. 1, *The Lord's Prayer in the Early Church* (Cambridge, 1891, repr. Nendeln/Liechtenstein, 1967), p. 1.

and the prophets the rulers of the synagogue invited them to speak. Nothing loth, Paul addressed a powerful message to the Jews and god-fearers, that is to say, proselytes. These were divided, some for and some against, but the next sabbath almost the whole city came to hear what Paul and Barnabas had to say. The hard-line Jews were disturbed by the apparent success, and denounced the Christian message in blasphemous language. At this point Paul and Barnabas declared, "It was necessary that the word of God should first have been spoken to you: but seeing ye put it from you, and judge yourselves unworthy of everlasting life (? did they), lo we turn to the Gentiles" (*Acts* 13: 46). This meant, of course, the Gentiles of that city and was not a final break with the Jews, for that final break did not come in Paul's lifetime. The Gentiles proved more receptive.

The theme was repeated with variations whenever Paul went to places with a Jewish population. At Thessalonica on the second journey the Jews were moved with envy and suborned "certain lewd fellows of the baser sort" to assault Paul and his host Jason (*Acts* 17: 5). At Corinth Paul began by testifying to the Jews that Jesus was Christ, but when they opposed and blasphemed he declared: "Your blood be upon your own heads; I am clean: from henceforth I will go unto the Gentiles"; and he became the guest of Justus in a house adjoining the synagogue (*Acts* 18: 5-7). Nevertheless among his converts was Crispus, the chief ruler of the synagogue. (It must have caused such a stir as when the chief rabbi of Rome announced his conversion to Christianity a few years back.) At Ephesus Paul managed to survive for three months disputing in the synagogue, but when opposition became too strong he betook himself to the school of Tyrannus for two years [26] (*Acts* 19: 8-9).

What was Paul's manner of approach to his audiences? It cannot be put better than in his own words.

"Unto the Jews I became as a Jew, that I might gain the Jews; to them that are under the law, as under the law, that I might gain them that are under the law. To them that are without law, as without law (being not without law to God but under the law to Christ), that I might gain them that are without law. To the weak

---

[26] The Western text as found in D, the Latin Vulgate and other witnesses adds the interesting detail that he taught in the lecture room of Tyrannus from the fifth to the tenth hour, that is, from 11 a.m. to 4 p.m. by our measurement. Tyrannus would himself have used it up to the fifth hour, when the day's work normally ceased. This is one of the credible details strengthening the supposition that D contains a later revision of *Acts*.

I became as weak, that I might gain the weak; I am made all things to all men, that I might by all means save some" (*1 Cor.* 9: 20–22).

In other words, Paul adapted his message to his audience. To the Jews he could be as crabbed an interpreter of the scriptures as any rabbi, to the sophisticated Athenians he could give a polished philosophical address embellished by a quotation from a Greek astronomical poet hardly better known then than he is today.[27] Whether to Jews or to Gentiles, to the intellectual or the hedonists, to proconsuls or to slaves, his addresses as they have come down to us were carefully prepared and skilfully tailored to the measurements of his hearers. The impression left by Luke's narrative is that the Athenian address was a failure in that it produced few converts, and Paul has himself contributed to that impression; but, if so, it was a failure on the part of the audience rather than on the part of the missionary. If Paul's careful address on that occasion could not convince, it was unlikely that any other approach would have won the hearts of that urbane but shallow collection of Epicureans and Stoics always waiting to tell or to hear some new thing (*Acts* 17: 18, 21). When he left Athens for Corinth—a very different city whose name had provided a slang word for loose living (*korinthiazesthai* = to fornicate)—he adopted a different tone which was far more successful in its results, "I, brethren, when I came to you, came not with excellency of speech or of wisdom, declaring unto you the testimony of God. For I determined not to know anything among you, save Jesus Christ and him crucified" (*1 Cor.* 2: 1–2). It looks like a confession by Paul that his approach to the Athenians was wrong; but if in the middle of the Areopagus he had proclaimed only "Jesus Christ and him crucified" it would probably have failed just as much as proclaiming "Jesus Christ and him raised from the dead". It was the over-subtle audience that was at fault, that at Corinth was more malleable material.

But can we be sure that in the speeches in *Acts* we have Paul's actual words? They occupy a substantial part of the narrative. If the author was Luke, Paul's travelling companion, and his companion in imprisonment at Rome, there would be nothing surprising in substantial verbal accuracy. He would himself have heard some of the speeches as delivered, such as the moving farewell at Miletus to the elders of Ephesus, and he would have

---

[27] Aratus, *Phaenomena*, 5, "For we also are his offspring", quoted in *Acts* 17: 28.

been told of others by those who heard them or even by Paul himself. As a physician he would be trained to a certain degree of scientific precision and probably made notes. Even without notes the memory or tale of what so gripping a speaker as Paul had said would never fade. Some who heard David Lloyd George's peroration at the Queen's Hall, London, on 21st September 1914 can still repeat it to this day, over sixty years after the event. The memory of what the same orator said in the House of Commons on 18th June 1936, on the abandonment of sanctions against Fascist Italy, or what Winston Churchill said in the same place on 5th October 1938 on the Munich settlement, not to mention such war-time speeches of his as I heard, is imperishably engraved in my own mind and does not need *Hansard* to bring them back. If we can thus remember what our own statesmen said in our youth, is it surprising that Paul's hearers did not forget what he had said on memorable occasions? He clearly made a powerful impression on his audiences. The pagan people of Lystra on his first journey gave him a name corresponding to the Greek god Hermes because he was "the chief speaker" (*Acts* 14: 12).[28]

There is a parallel worthy of study. Thucydides in his history of the Peloponnesian war gives a large number of speeches by men to whom he stood in the temporal relationship as that in which Luke stood to Paul. He wrote before 400 BC about events that had taken place between 431 and 404, and he laid down the principles governing the composition of these speeches. "As regards the speeches made by different men, either when they were about to engage in hostilities or were already involved, it is hard for me to remember with accuracy what I myself heard or for those who from other sources have supplied me with reports. Therefore what each of the various speakers said has been given in the words which, as it seemed to me, they would employ on the occasions in question, but I have followed as closely as possible the general sense of what was really said" (1. xxii. 1).

The implication of this avowal is that the speeches truly reflect what was said but that their verbal accuracy should not be pressed. Commenting on it a great classical scholar, H. T. Wade-Gery, while conceding that some of the speeches cannot have been delivered exactly as recorded, observes: "It is yet dangerous to treat the speeches as free fiction; their dramatic truth was combined with the greatest degree of literal truth of which Thucydides

---

[28] We need not take *au pied de la lettre* Paul's self-depreciating remark, "his speech contemptible" (*2 Cor.* 10: 10).

was capable. He tried to re-create real occasions."[29] We may fairly apply these words to Luke writing some 460 years later than Thucydides. As an educated Greek he probably knew his Thucydides, and in writing the speeches in *Acts* he may well have had Thucydides' words in mind. His speeches accurately reflect, even if they may not in detail accurately record, what Paul said on specific occasions.

How did Paul write his letters during his missionary journeys? He was not singular in the ancient world in dictating them to amanuenses. Indeed, the practice of dictation was even commoner among the great writers of antiquity than it is among their successors to-day, perhaps because the art of writing was then more difficult and was often entrusted to slaves or professionals. The subscriptions found in some manuscripts tell us that the letter was written by so-and-so from such-and-such a place, but these subscriptions are not conclusive evidence as they are sometimes obviously deductions at a fairly late date from internal evidence or clearly wrong. We can happily be confident about the most important item in the correspondence. The final chapter of the *Epistle to the Romans* makes clear that it was carried to Rome by Phoebe, a deaconess of the church at Cenchreae, the port of Corinth (*Rom.* 16: 1–2), and the letter must have been written at one of the few periods when Paul would have had the leisure to compose such a carefully-reasoned piece—at Corinth on his second journey; into the salutations the amanuensis has put his own greeting—"I Tertius, who wrote this epistle, salute you in the Lord" (*Rom.* 16: 22), and it is possible that Gaius, with whom Paul was then staying and whom he had personally baptized (*1 Cor.* 1: 14), and Erastus the chamberlain of the city and Quartus also added their greetings in their own hand (*Rom.* 16: 23). On one occasion Paul himself seized the stylus from his amanuensis to add his greeting, "The salutation of *me* Paul with mine own hand" (*1 Cor.* 16: 21) and he may have personally written also the three sentences that follow. On another occasion when Paul himself took the pen he observed, "You see with what ungainly characters (literally, "many-coloured characters", but that can hardly be the sense, and we have to resort to a secondary meaning, the Authorized Version not being far out, "how large a letter") I have written unto you with mine own hand" (*Gal.* 6: 11). Though other men of small stature have been known

---

[29] *Oxford Classical Dictionary*, 2nd ed. (Oxford, 1970), *s.v.* "Thucydides", p. 1068.

to use a large script, may this be corroborative evidence that Paul suffered from some eye trouble? It has been suggested that his failure to recognize the high priest, Ananias, except dimly as a "whited wall", when brought before the Sanhedrin may indicate some defect of vision (*Acts* 23: 1–5).

Be that as it may, *Galatians* is universally recognized to have been one of the earliest of Paul's letters. It is rivalled only by the two letters to the Thessalonians, which some consider to be earlier. *1 Thess.* 3: 1–2 informs us that Paul sent Timothy from Athens to strengthen the newly-founded church in Thessalonica, which he had been forced to leave rather hurriedly on his second journey. It will be recalled that after leaving Philippi Paul had some success at Thessalonica, but a section of the Jews, moved with envy, suborned "certain lewd fellows of the baser sort" to assault the house of Jason where he and Silas were staying, and the brethren thought it prudent to send them on to Beroea; there they found an even greater receptivity, both among Jews and Greeks, including women of social standing, but their Jewish opponents in Thessalonica stirred up trouble there also, and Paul, leaving Silas and Timothy with a command to follow him as quietly as possible, went on to Athens (*Acts* 17: 1–15). It was probably there, as the subscriptions say, or possibly a little later during the longer stay at Corinth, that the two epistles to the Thessalonians—"ensamples to all that believe in Macedonia and Achaia (*1 Thess.* 1: 7)—were written.

It may have been during his long stay in Corinth that news reached Paul of the backsliding of his Galatian converts, misled by emissaries from Jerusalem who taught that full observance of the Jewish law, including circumcision, was necessary even for Gentiles. The subscription, that the letter was written from Rome, is clearly without foundation, but a strong case can be made out for saying that it was written between the first and second journeys while Paul was at Antioch. The crucial fact is that the letter shows no awareness of the Council of Jerusalem, as we have already noticed. Some modern scholars have taken this as proof of the unhistorical character of the narrative in *Acts*. It is simpler, and more scientific, to suppose that *Galatians* was written before the Council, which finally put an end to the controversy about how far the requirements of the Jewish law were binding on Gentile Christians. The sequence would be as follows: Paul and Barnabas made their first converts in Galatia—at Pisidian Antioch, Iconium, Lystra and Derbe (*Acts* 13: 14—14: 24). They returned to Antioch, where they "abode long time with the disciples" (*Acts*

14: 28). While they were there those who insisted on full compliance with the Jewish law opened a major offensive (*Acts* 15: 1). Even Peter and Barnabas felt obliged to withdraw from the progressive courses on which they had embarked, and when Peter had occasion to come to Antioch Paul withstood him to his face (*Gal.* 2: 11-14). But what really incensed Paul was the news that the Judaizers had been at work among his own Galatian converts, and in a flame of passion he wrote to them the first of all his letters. "O foolish Galatians, who hath bewitched you?" (*Gal.* 3: 1). The matter clearly had to be brought to an issue, and Paul and Barnabas were authorized to go to Jerusalem to settle the matter once and for all with the apostles and elders. These agreed to convene the gathering which has rightly come to be known as the Council of Jerusalem, for it has all the marks of being the first general council of the Church. Under the presidency of James, with Peter playing a leading part, the council came to a sensible compromise which they embodied in a letter sent to the churches of Antioch, Syria and Cilicia: "It seemed good to the Holy Ghost, and to us, to lay upon you no greater burden than these necessary things; that ye abstain from meats offered to idols, and from blood, and from things strangled and from fornication" (*Acts* 15: 28-29). (The Western text omits "from things strangled", and some texts omit "from fornication", and there is argument whether "from blood" is a ritual prohibition as a ban on homicide, but the essential point is that circumcision was not to be required of Gentile converts.) Well satisfied, Paul now back at Antioch was soon itching to see his Galatian converts again, and started on his second journey; he took with him Silas, who had been commissioned with Judas to bear the letter from the apostles and elders, and they gladly delivered the council's decrees to the local churches (*Acts* 16: 4). When they arrived at Lystra there was commended to him a disciple who was to be one of his greatest lieutenants—Timothy. Paul was impressed and persuaded Timothy to join him; and because Timothy's mother was a Jewess, though his father was a Greek, he circumcised him (*Acts* 16: 1-3) in order to avoid needless controversy and to show how punctilious he was in keeping his part in the compromise reached at the council. On his second visit to Jerusalem he had not circumcised Titus, who was wholly Greek (*Gal.* 2: 3).

Paul's first letter to the Corinthians was clearly written from Ephesus, where he proposed to stay until Pentecost and where "a great door and effectual is opened unto me, and there are many adversaries" (*1 Cor.* 16: 8-9), and he added "the churches of

Asia salute you" (*1 Cor.* 16: 19). Aquila and Priscilla were with him (*ibid.*), which agrees with Luke's account in *Acts* 18: 26. Stephanas and Fortunatus and Achaicus had just arrived from Corinth, and no doubt they confirmed the news of divisions in the church at Corinth which so grieved Paul, news already brought by the household of Chloe (*1 Cor.* 1: 11), some saying they were of Paul, some of Apollos, some of Cephas and some of Christ (*1 Cor.* 1: 12). We know from Luke's gripping narrative something about the adversaries in Ephesus, where the mob was stirred up by Demetrius, a maker of silver images, into howling for two hours on end, "Great is Artemis of the Ephesians" (*Acts* 19: 34), and only the tact of the town clerk saved an ugly outcome. Perhaps this is what Paul had in mind when he asked rhetorically, "If, humanly speaking, I have fought with wild beasts at Ephesus, what benefit is that to me?" (*1* Cor. 15: 32). It is unlikely that he meant to imply he was thrown into the arena, or that he would have survived if he had been.

The second epistle to the Corinthians, as we know it, includes portions of two or possibly three letters, and we cannot assert that "it" was written at any one place. One definite fact that emerges is that when 2 *Cor.* 16 was written Paul had already been twice to Corinth and was proposing to pay a third visit.

What happened to Paul's letters when they reached their destination? From that to the Colossians we know that it was publicly read to the congregation for whom it was written. "When this epistle is read among you, cause that it be read also in the church of the Laodiceans; and that ye likewise read the epistle from Laodicea" (*Col.* 4: 16). We may imagine the excitement when the bearer of a letter from Paul arrived and the eagerness with which all would assemble in the house of one of their number to hear it. The passage quoted suggests that such letters were also read in neighbouring churches, and that Paul wrote a letter to the Laodiceans which has not survived. In view of this widespread reading, it is probable that the letters were copied immediately. Their authoritative nature, and probably their literary and theological qualities, were immediately recognized (*2 Cor.* 10: 10); and it is not surprising that by the time *2 Peter* was written, at some date in the second century in all probability, there was already a corpus of Pauline letters placed on the level of Holy Writ (*2 Pet.* 3: 15–16).

Was Paul as dominating a figure in the early history of Christianity as *Acts* represents him to be? St. Luke's portrait of Paul is brilliantly executed. It is the portrait of a man who is dreaded as the chief persecutor of the Church, undergoes a spectacular conversion, as is emphasized by the thrice-told tale (*Acts* 9: 1–22, 22: 3–16, 26: 9–20), finds it difficult to win acceptance as a Christian convert, but by the force of his personality gradually takes pre-eminence over all other Christian leaders, so much so that he successfully imposes his views upon the early Christian community, more than any other man being responsible for turning a Jewish sect into a universal Church, and carries its message over the whole eastern half of the Roman Empire to the very capital. When the church in Antioch sent forth its first mission, it was Barnabas who was the leader and Saul, as he was then known, was secondary. If Barnabas had not given Saul his patronage, the latter would probably have remained ineffective in Cilicia for many more years. When the church at Antioch sent out its mission the order was "Barnabas and Saul", and it was to Cyprus, the birthplace of Barnabas (*Acts* 4: 36) that the mission first went. In that island the proconsul, Sergius Paulus, summoned "Barnabas and Saul" before him, but it was the latter's handling of the proconsul's astrologer, Hetoimos,[30] "the resourceful one", that converted the Roman, and when the mission left his seat at New Paphos the mission had become "Paul and his company". At Antioch in Pisidia it is Paul who preaches the great sermon to the Jews, and when the congregation breaks up it is "Paul and Barnabas" whom many of the Jews and proselytes follow, and "Paul and Barnabas" who wax bold and turn to the Gentiles and are expelled. At Lystra Barnabas is honoured by the well-meaning barbarians with the title of the chief of the gods, but that is because they recognize in Paul the chief speaker, equivalent to Hermes, and for the moment, but only for the moment, the order is again "Barnabas and Paul". On their return to Antioch it is "Paul and Barnabas" who are sent to Jerusalem to persuade the apostles and elders not to fetter the Gentile converts with the ritual commandments of the Jewish law. When they get there the order again becomes "Barnabas and Paul", for Barnabas had

[30] This seems another case where the reading of the Western text is to be preferred. The name originally given to the *magos* is Bar-jesus and at the next mention (*Acts* 13: 8) Luke says according to most manuscripts: "Elymas the *magos* (for so is his name by interpretation)." It is a mistake on the part of the commentators, misled by the proximity of the word, to suppose that *magos*, "astrologer" (A.V. "sorcerer") is meant to be a translation of Elymas, and desperate efforts have been made to find some Hebrew meaning in Elymas. Clearly Elymas is intended to be a Greek rendering of some Hebrew name prefixed to Bar-jesus, "son of Jesus" (not Jesus Christ, of course—Jesus was a common name), but it is not Greek whereas the reading of D. Hetoimas = Hetoimos, "the resourceful", makes good sense.

been well known to the church in Jerusalem from its early days, and although when they have substantially formed their point of view the Council decide to send chosen men with "Paul and Barnabas" to convey their decrees, their actual letter gives the order as "our beloved Barnabas and Paul". On their return to Antioch, it is Paul who proposes to Barnabas a second mission, and by this time he is so sure of himself that he would not agree to take with them Barnabas's cousin, John Mark,[31] who for some reason had left them at Perga[32] in Pamphylia on the first journey (*Acts* 13: 13); and he and Barnabas went their separate ways, Barnabas taking Mark to Cyprus again and Paul taking Silas into Asia. From that point we hear no more of Barnabas in *Acts*—though he is honourably mentioned by Paul—(*1 Cor.* 9: 6, *Col.* 4: 10)—and the narrative is concentrated entirely upon St. Paul and his companion.

There is nothing accidental in *Acts*—the most careful work ever composed outside a purely scientific treatise—and it is not to be doubted that St. Luke's choice of order is deliberate. At first it is "Barnabas and Saul", then there is uncertainty about the order, but eventually the order becomes "Paul and Barnabas", and finally Paul alone.

It is unlikely that Barnabas faded out of the Christian picture entirely after his second missionary journey to Cyprus, and still harder to believe that Peter, who plays such a prominent part in the first half of *Acts*, had no further role to play after the Council of Jerusalem. He certainly went to Rome, though this is nowhere recorded in any early writing, and the archaeological evidence is strong that his body is buried there. And what of John the son of Zebedee, who is hardly mentioned in *Acts*? Undoubtedly at a later date he was the head of the Ephesian church which Paul had for all practical purposes founded (see Note 23 above). The other apostles, too, could hardly have been inactive, and there is probably a stratum of truth in the traditions about their journeyings. Then there are St. Paul's numerous fellow-workers, who cannot have been the shadowy figures that they now appear to us for lack

---

[31] Probably Mark had expected a simple journey to Cyprus and back, and could not or would not accept the change of plan and a mission to the interior of Asia Minor. It is pleasing to think that Paul became reconciled to him in later years (*Col.* 4: 10 and probably *Philem* 1: 24, *2 Tim.* 4: 11). As the interpreter of Peter (so Papias) he would have been a link between the two great apostles.

[32] Educated Greek though he was, Luke may not have recognized in Perga its chief title to fame in modern eyes: it was the birthplace of Apollonius who had so powerfully developed the theory of conic sections in the 3rd century BC.

of documentation. As stated above, Aquila and Priscilla, Apollos (did he write the *Epistle to the Hebrews?*), Silas, Timothy, Titus and Epaphras at least must have been considerable figures in their day, but Paul steals the show. This is not to accuse Luke of inaccuracy. Paul was his hero, and like other historians and biographers he selects the material that suits his purpose.

And what was that purpose? One purpose, it has already been hinted, was to show Paul as favourably disposed towards the Roman Empire in view of his impending trial in the capital. If we look at *Acts* from the angle of this hypothesis, the book becomes far more intelligible than would otherwise be the case.

The work is dedicated, like the third gospel, to Theophilus, and the title given to him in the gospel, *kratiste*, "most excellent" (*Luke* 1: 3) implies that he belonged to the equestrian order, or possibly was a senator; who he was we do not know, for Theophilus, "beloved of God", would be a name given to him at or since his baptism and conceals his Latin name, but the dedication strikes the key-note of *Acts*.

When Paul begins his missionary journeys, the first convert claimed for him by Luke is none other than a Roman proconsul—Sergius Paulus,[33] the *anthupatos* (Luke, careful as ever, gives the correct technical term for proconsul) of Cyprus (*Acts* 13: 7). The proconsul, already well disposed—for he had summoned Barnabas and Saul to his presence—when he saw Paul mete out to his astrologer the same treatment that he had himself received at the Lord's hands outside Damascus—"believed, being astonished at the doctrine of the Lord" (*Acts* 13: 12). It is as though Luke is saying to the Roman jury, "You see how the accused has from the outset been the friend of our rulers".

At this point Luke introduces a subtle but significant change in nomenclature. "Then Saul", he says, "who is also called Paul" (*Acts* 13: 9), and henceforth the apostle, hitherto known by his Hebrew name Saul, is always referred to by his Roman name Paul save only when recounting his conversion. It was a common custom among the mixed population of the east Mediterranean for Semites to have a second Greek or Latin name, and frequently the main reason in the choice of the second name was that it

---

[33] He may be the Paulus mentioned in a contemporary Cypriot inscription, but this is not certain.

sounded like the Semitic original.[34] In the apostle's case the second name may have been appropriate, for the Latin "Paulus" means "small", and he has himself recorded that, according to some, his bodily presence was weak (*2 Cor.* 10: 10). For what it is worth there is also the evidence of the *Acts of St. Paul* that he was "a man of small stature".[35] Whatever the appropriateness, it would appear that from this point onwards by the choice of name Luke wishes to emphasize his Latinity.[36]

Paul's missionary journeys began in the province of Cilicia and Syria and, after Cyprus, continued in Lycia-Pamphylia, Galatia, Asia, Macedonia and Achaia, with side glances at Pontus and at Illyricum. The spirit suffered him not to go into Bithynia (*Acts* 16: 17), then joined in one province with Pontus, where Aquila had been born (*Acts* 18: 2), but he could proudly proclaim that "from Jerusalem and round about unto Illyricum I have fully preached the gospel of Christ" (*Rom.* 15: 19).[37] It is significant that Luke uses the Greek forms of the Latin names of the provinces. He could have used other geographical units, and in one place he does speak of Phrygia (*Acts* 16: 6), then divided between Asia and Galatia, but it is no accident that in general he uses the Roman political units, just as a historian to-day might be careful to place Doncaster in South Yorkshire rather than in the West Riding. It is one of his small but significant acts of deference to the Roman power.

It was at Philippi in Macedonia—a colony, as Luke so accurately observes—during the second journey, that Paul first claimed his Roman citizenship so far as we know—though this must have come out in conversation with Sergius Paulus. He had cast a

---

[34] This was recognized by C. S. Clermont-Ganneau, *Recueil d'archéologie orientale* I (Paris, 1886), p. 186 and has been developed by F. Rosenthal, *Die Sprache der palmyrenischen Inschriften* (Leipzig, 1936), pp. 93-94. I am indebted for these references to G. J. Toomer, "The Mathematician Zenodorus" in *Greek, Roman and Byzantine Studies,* Vol. 13 (1972), pp. 181-183, where the practice is also discussed.

[35] Hennecke-Schneemelcher, *New Testament Apocrypha,* Vol. 2, p. 354.

[36] As a Roman citizen Paul would have had three names—*praenomen, nomen* and *cognomen,* of which Paulus would be the cognomen. The proconsul, for example, might have been Marcus Sergius Paulus. It is unlikely that the apostle began to call himself Paul after the proconsul as the change of name is mentioned before the latter's conversion, or even that he began to use it in honour of the latter's conversion. The simple explanation is that he always had the second name and that in the Greek-speaking world it was natural to use it.

[37] This does not necessarily mean that he had entered Illyricum, though he may have done so; it would have been sufficient if he had reached the border.

"spirit of divination" out of a girl who had brought her masters much gain thereby, and when they saw that their hope of gain was gone they stirred up the multitude and dragged Paul and Silas before the Roman magistrates, alleging that they taught customs "which are not lawful for us to receive, neither to observe, being Romans" (*Acts* 16: 21). The magistrates ordered Paul and Silas to be beaten and put them into gaol. By the Lex Iulia [38] enacted in the reign of Augustus it was not lawful to flog a Roman citizen, but Paul and Silas accepted their punishment without disclosing their citizenship.[39] When an earthquake shook the prison to its foundations during the night, and the prisoners might have escaped, the magistrates would have released them from custody, but Paul turned the tables on them by saying—we can still hear his mocking voice across the centuries—"They have beaten us openly uncondemned, being Romans, and have cast us into prison: and now do they thrust us out privily? nay verily, but let them come themselves and fetch us out" (*Acts* 16: 37). Luke adds that the magistrates feared when they heard that Paul and Silas were Romans, and well they might, for *Civis Romanus sum* was a powerful saying and a Roman citizen could not be unlawfully treated with impunity. The magistrates came in person and implored them to leave.

Paul was proud of his Roman citizenship,[40] and on occasion it stood him in good stead. When the Jews would have lynched him in Jerusalem for allegedly bringing a Gentile, the Ephesian Trophimus, into the Temple, and the commander of the Roman garrison, Claudius Lysias, rescued him and proposed to interrogate

---

[38] See below, note 43.

[39] This would be one of the three occasions mentioned in *2 Cor.* 11: 25 when Paul states that he was "beaten with rods". The other two occasions are unknown, unless we accept the story of Thecla in the *Acts of St. Paul* (see below), in which case one would have been at Iconium. These beatings are distinguished from the five occasions, all unknown, when he received from the Jews "forty stripes save one" (*2 Cor.* 11: 24). These punishments could lawfully be imposed by the Jewish authorities for religious offences both in the Holy Land and in the Diaspora. The thirty-nine lashes just kept within the limit of forty laid down in *Deut.* 25: 3. The stoning to which Paul refers in *2 Cor.* 11: 25 would be that recorded in *Acts* 14: 19 at Lystra, but this was an act of mob violence not formally ordered by the synagogue authorities—and happily not carried so far as that of Stephen. The three shipwrecks mentioned in the same passage are not otherwise recorded.

[40] It may be asked why Paul did not claim it at Philippi before he was beaten, and the answer may be to show his readiness to suffer for Christ. This may also be the explanation of the two other occasions when he was "beaten with rods", or he may have wished to identify himself with other victims who could not claim Roman citizenship.

him by scourging—a common enough practice with slaves and non-Romans—Paul coolly asked the centurion, "Is it lawful for you to scourge a man that is a Roman, and uncondemned?" (*Acts* 22: 25).[41] The centurion promptly reported to the commander, "Take heed what thou doest: for this man is a Roman". The commander's interest was at once aroused, and the famous exchange took place:

"Tell me, art thou a Roman? He said, Yea. And the commander of the garrison answered, With a great sum obtained I this freedom. And Paul said, But I was born free."

Born a Roman citizen! Naturally the commander became apprehensive. There has been much speculation how Paul's father (or some ancestor) acquired his Roman citizenship. The suggestion that Pompey in his settlement of the eastern provinces in the sixties BC transferred a group of Jewish prisoners to Tarsus and set them free has been shown to be due to a misunderstanding of Roman custom.[42] Some have liked to think that the citizenship was acquired in BC 41 when Cleopatra sailed up the river Cydnus to Tarsus with the object of captivating Mark Antony, as indeed she did; no doubt many were given Roman citizenship to mark the occasion, and if Paul's father was among them the apostle would have been Marcus Antonius Paulus. Others have preferred to think it was a few years earlier when Cicero was governor of Cilicia, of which Tarsus was the capital, in which case the apostle would have been Marcus Tullius Paulus—but it is idle to indulge in such fancies with no solid basis of documentation.

Did Paul know Latin as well as Hebrew, Aramaic and Greek? It is more than likely that so well-read a man knew some Latin, and the authorities liked to extend the knowledge of Latin, which was the official language of the army; but it was not a condition of citizenship and there is no evidence that Paul had any Latin. He conversed with Claudius Lysias in Greek: "Canst thou speak Greek?" said the Roman commander in some surprise (*Acts* 21: 37)—and Greek was the *lingua franca* of the eastern provinces and the official language of public administration in Syria and Palestine.

---

[41] There would, as A. N. Sherwin-White observes, *op. cit.*, pp. 149–150, have been nothing in Paul's appearance to indicate his citizenship. At Rome the Roman citizen would have been known by his *toga*, but this is not likely to have been worn in the eastern provinces. A Roman citizen by birth could have produced a copy of the *professio* or registration of his birth, but these certificates were probably kept in family archives and not carried about.

[42] See A. N. Sherwin-White, *op. cit.*, pp. 151–152.

What is certain is that Paul was proud of being a Roman citizen and knew both the duties and the privileges of citizenship. It was in this knowledge that he made his "appeal to Caesar", in the technical language of Roman law his *provocatio ad Caesarem*, that is to say, he insisted on his right as a Roman citizen to be tried in the imperial court at Rome.[43]

Why did Paul decide to appeal to Caesar? He had on one occasion at least experience of the fairness of Roman provincial justice. For when the Jews sought to arraign Paul before Lucius Junius Gallio, newly arrived at Corinth as proconsul of Achaia, he quickly decided that there was no case to answer and dismissed the suit.[44] What is more, when the frustrated Jews turned on the leader of the synagogue, Sosthenes, and beat him before the judgment seat Gallio ignored the action.

After his rescue from lynching in Jerusalem, Paul was again to meet the Roman power in the person of Antonius Felix, procurator of Judaea. On the death of Herod Agrippa in 44, Palestine had been made a minor imperial province and Felix was its third procurator. He is a well-documented figure in Roman history, the brother of the influential freedman Pallas, but his rule in Judaea

---

[43] The prime authority for the process of *provocatio* is *Lex Iulia de vi publica* as cited by Ulpian in *De officio proconsulis* and in the *Sententiae* of the fourth-century jurist Paulus. The text in Ulpian reads: *Lege Iulia de vi publica tenetur qui cum imperium potestatem haberet civem Romanum adversus provocationem necaverit verberaverit iussertive quid fieri aut quid in collum iniecerit ut torqueretur*. A passage cited from Marcian adds: *Lege Iulia de vi cavetur ne quis reum vinciat impediatve quominus Romae intra certum tempus adsit*. The text in the *Sententiae Pauli* adds: *qui . . . condemnaverit inve publica vincula duci iusserit*. As summarized by A. N. Sherwin-White, *op. cit.*, pp. 58-59: "These clauses of the *Lex Iulia de vi* protected the Roman citizen who invoked the ancient right of *provocatio*, from summary punishment, execution and torture without trial, from private or public arrest, and from actual trial by magistrates outside Italy. They are to be understood in connexion with the *ordo* system, which had created for Roman citizens a method of trial by jury at Rome for statutory offences. Against this there was no *provocatio*. The citation from Ulpian proves only the protection against physical punishment, whether as an act of *coercitio* or by way of executing sentence. But the fragment in the *Sententiae Pauli* indicates that *provocatio* protected a man from trial and sentence: *qui . . . condemnaverit.*" See also the valuable essay by A. H. M. Jones, "I appeal unto Caesar", in *Studies presented to D. M. Robinson*, pp. 918ff, reprinted in *Studies in Roman Government*, pp. 67ff.

[44] "And when Paul was about to open his mouth Gallio said unto the Jews, If it were a matter of wrong or wicked lewdness, O ye Jews, reason would that I should bear with you: But if it be a question of words and names, and of your law, look ye to it: for I will be no judge of such matters. And he drave them from the judgment seat" (*Acts* 18: 14-16).

was unfortunate and in due course he was recalled[45] and would have been executed but for the intercession of his brother. When Paul was brought before him at Caesarea by a military escort, he behaved correctly, reading the documents and holding a preliminary hearing but deferring judgment until Claudius Lysias should arrive in person. In the meantime he allowed Paul a considerable degree of liberty and commanded the centurion who had charge of him to allow free access to visitors. He frequently sent for Paul, but Luke hints at a base motive—that he was hoping for a bribe to set him free. The upshot was that Paul was still a prisoner when Felix was recalled and Porcius Festus took his place. He had already been in custody for two years.

Porcius Festus showed greater expedition. Three days after his arrival at Caesarea he went to Jerusalem and listened to the charges brought by the high priest and other leading Jews. They tried to persuade him to send Paul back to Jerusalem, planning to ambush and kill him on the way, but Festus did not fall into the trap, and required them to bring their charges in Caesarea. After ten days in Jerusalem he returned to his capital, and the very next day tried the case. Paul's defence was "Neither against the law of the Jews, neither against the temple, nor yet against Caesar, have I offended anything at all" (*Acts* 25: 8). Festus, "willing to do the Jews a pleasure", then asked if he was prepared to have the case adjourned to Jerusalem. It was at this point that Paul made his appeal to Caesar. No doubt Festus thought that he could try the case just as impartially in one place as the other, and as the alleged offences had been committed in Jerusalem the evidence might be more readily available there. But Paul knew the temper of the Jews, and even if he was not ambushed on the way the procurator might sit with assessors (his *concilium*) composed of the Sanhedrin or leading members thereof. Moreover, the charge of profaning the temple might be one on which the Jews could take charge of the trial themselves and lawfully sentence him to death. Perhaps a sub-conscious wish to get to Rome, even as a prisoner, may have mingled with his other reasons. He claimed his right to be tried at Caesar's judgment seat. "Hast thou appealed unto Caesar?" said Festus, "unto Caesar shalt thou go". But he

---

[45] It is unfortunate that discrepancies between Tacitus and Josephus do not permit his period of office to be determined.

could not be sent immediately. A little later, Agrippa II and his consort Bernice arrived from their tetrarchy to pay their respects to Porcius Festus, and the procurator invited him to hear Paul. "It is not the manner of the Romans", said Festus, "to deliver any man to die, before that he which is accused have the accusers face to face and have licence to answer for himself concerning the crime laid against him"—Luke's narrative is shot through with such encomiums on Roman legal administration.

To Agrippa Festus gave as his reason for suggesting an adjournment of the trial to Jerusalem that the accusations turned out to be no criminal charges but "certain questions against him of their own religion, and of one Jesus, who was dead, whom Paul affirmed to be alive" (*Acts* 25: 19). He could find no cause of death in Paul, and perhaps Agrippa could help him in making his report to Rome. After a memorable interview with Paul, Agrippa concurred. "This man might have been set at liberty if he had not appealed unto Caesar" (*Acts* 26: 32). Such statements could only make a favourable impression when read in Rome, as Luke on our hypothesis intended them to be.[46]

Paul had for some time longed to see Rome. To the Christians in Rome he wrote the longest and most carefully composed of all his letters, and towards the end of it he said, "Whensoever I take my journey into Spain, I will come to you; for I trust to see you in my journey, and to be brought on my way thitherward by you, if first I be somewhat filled with your company. But now I go unto Jerusalem to minister to the saints" (*Rom.* 15: 24–25). Luke records the same purpose at what is obviously about the same time—at Ephesus on the third journey just before the uproar caused by Demetrius: "Paul purposed in the spirit, when he had passed through Macedonia and Achaia, to go to Jerusalem, saying, After I have been there I must also see Rome" (*Acts* 19: 21). In the end he saw it in a way that he did not intend—though some have advanced the theory that he appealed to Caesar, and perhaps

---

[46] A. N. Sherwin-White, *op. cit.*, pp. 68–69, has this observation to make after his close study of the text of *Acts*: "The account of the trial before Festus and Felix is thus sufficiently accurate in all its details. In its references to *provocatio* it is in accord with what is otherwise known of the practice in the first century AD. What is equally important is the fact that the author does not confuse *provocatio* with the procedure of the late Empire known as *appellatio*. . . . The study of *provocatio* in Acts thus provides a useful chronological countercheck in more ways than one."

deliberately courted imprisonment, for the purpose of travelling to Rome, and that at the expense of the State! As soon as he was rescued by the *tribunus militum* from the ugly mob that threatened to pull him to pieces in Jerusalem he knew that he would realize his ambition. For "the night following, the Lord stood by him, and said, Be of good cheer, Paul: for as thou hast testified of me in Jerusalem, so must thou bear witness also at Rome" (*Acts* 23: 11).

Rome, the *urbs aeterna*, the mistress of the world, obviously played a big part in Paul's imagination. The world has, indeed, never seen a polity more remarkable than the Roman Empire. After the convulsions of the civil wars had been ended by the genius of Augustus, peace rested upon the whole area bounded by the Atlantic ocean in the west and the Euphrates-Tigris in the east and between the Sahara desert in the south and the Rhine-Danube in the north. Within this vast area the reign of law prevailed and the arts flourished. Roads, the like of which was not to be seen until the eighteenth century, connected the capital with the most distant parts. Paul was deeply conscious of the merits of this unique polity. He carried his message along its roads under the protection of its proconsuls and legates. When he wrote, "The powers that be are ordained of God" (*Rom.* 13: 1) he was writing to Romans about the Roman Empire, and he meant what he said. Just as Dante saw in its successor the Holy Roman Empire a divinely appointed agent, just as surely Paul discerned in the Roman Empire an instrument in God's purpose for mankind. Therefore he told the Romans, "Let every soul be subject unto the higher powers", and "Whosoever resisteth the power, resisteth the ordinance of God". Surely these words must have been produced in Paul's defence at Rome and could hardly have failed to win credibility for his plea of "Not guilty"!

In a sense Paul's voyage to Rome was a fourth missionary journey, for he seized every opportunity to convert—as Agrippa playfully retorted ("In a twinkling you would persuade me to act the Christian", *Acts* 26: 28). But we need not dwell on the details,

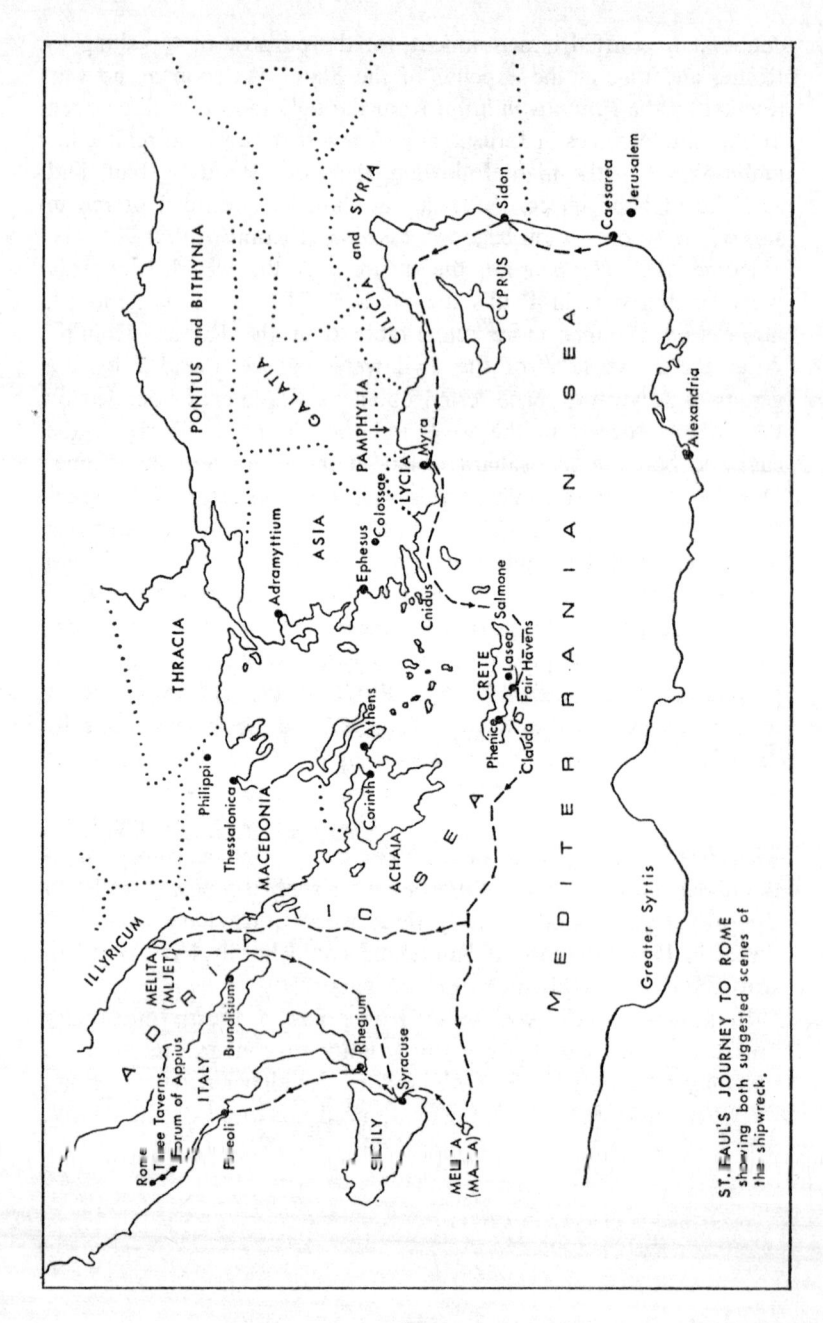

ST. PAUL'S JOURNEY TO ROME
showing both suggested scenes of
the shipwreck.

and one theory about the shipwreck is expounded in the next essay in this volume by Mr. Angus Acworth.[47]

What it is in place to mention here is that the island on which St. Paul was shipwrecked—for the fourth time—was a Roman possession, and Paul became friendly with the "chief man" of the island after curing his father of dysentery and a fever. (Did Luke the physician have a hand in the cure?) If the island was Mljet, it was part of the Roman province of Illyricum. If it was Malta, it was an ally of Rome governed from Sicily, and the title of *princeps* for its "chief man" is attested in inscriptions. His name is recorded by Luke as Poplios, which is the usual Greek transliteration of Publius. But Publius is a *praenomen,* and as the use of a *praenomen* alone is unusual Ramsay has suggested that it may be a rendering of the nomen Popilius.[48] There can be no doubt that once again Luke was at pains to convey the impression that Paul was on good terms with the representative of Roman authority, and that this picture corresponds with the truth. The people of the island are said to have honoured Paul and his friends with many honours and to have sent them on their way with such things as were necessary (*Acts* 28: 10).

When sailing was resumed at the end of the winter season— 7th February was the regular date—Paul was taken in an Alexandrian ship that had wintered in the island on his way to Rome, stopping at Syracuse, Rhegium (Reggio di Calabria) and Puteoli.

---

[47] A few notes from the writer's own interests may be added. (1) The fact that the storm-beaten vessel was "driven up and down in Adria" cannot be adduced as evidence (it is not, of course, so adduced by Mr. Acworth) one way or the other as Ptolemy only a hundred years later makes the Adriatic wash the western coast of Crete (Ptolemy, *Geography* III. 17. 1, *Claudii Ptolemaei Geographia,* C. F. A. Nobbe ed., p. 218. 12-13). (2) Of the two forms for the tempestuous wind given in the MSS. *euraquilo,* which is found in the Codex Sinaiticus, the Codex Alexandrinus, Codex Vaticanus, the Old Latin versions and the Latin Vulgate, the Palestine Syriac version and the Coptic versions, is much better attested than *euroclydon,* but as both forms occur only here in the Greek language we are left to guess. The classic place in Greek literature for a description of the winds is Aristotle, *Meteorologus* II. vi, 363a 21—365a 13, F. H. Fobes ed., or in the Loeb Library, H. D. P. Lee ed., pp. 186-199. Eurus blows from the winter sunrise, that is, east-south-east. Aquilo is not found in Aristotle, but in Latin authors the name means a north wind, or more exactly a north-east-north wind. The combination *euraquilo* ought therefore to mean a wind blowing about 15 degrees north of east. (3) I am bound to agree with Mr. Acworth that *syrtes* cannot possibly refer to the Great Syrtes some hundreds of miles away; it must refer to a local sandbank. (4) If Paul and his company spent the winter at Mljet, I should have expected them to be disembarked at Brundisium (the modern Brindisi), whence they could quickly have travelled to Rome by the Via Appia, instead of going to Syracuse.

[48] W. M. Ramsay, *St. Paul the Traveller and Roman Citizen,* p. 393.

At the last port they left the ship and stayed seven days, and Paul found a Christian congregation already there. News went ahead, and when the party, now travelling overland, arrived at the Forum of Appius and the near-by Three Taverns Paul found that a reception committee of Roman Christians had come to greet him. At Rome the centurion handed Paul into the custody of the commandant of the camp (*stratopedarchos*, A.V. "captain of the guard", *Acts* 28: 16). Paul would certainly have been entrusted to the Praetorian Guard, for that body regularly took charge of prisoners sent from the provinces; and by the *stratopedarchos* is probably meant the *princeps castrorum*, the chief administrator of the *officium* of the Praetorian Guard—its adjutant, as we might say.[49] Paul was not imprisoned in the normal sense of the word. He was "suffered to dwell by himself with a soldier that kept him" (*Acts* 28: 16), that is to say, he was placed under house arrest chained to a soldier. It was a house for which he, or more probably his friends, paid rent (*Acts* 28: 30), and he was allowed to receive visitors. As usual he began his missionary efforts with his fellow Jews, and convinced some, but not all, whereupon he once more proclaimed, "Be it known therefore unto you that the salvation of God is sent unto the Gentiles, and that they will hear it" (*Acts* 28: 28).

Paul dwelt a prisoner in this hired house for at least two years (*Acts* 28: 30). There is nothing surprising in the period. It is known from secular sources that the courts were very congested at that date, and time would be needed for his accusers to come from Jerusalem. It is a fair deduction from phrases in the *Epistle to the Ephesians*—"I Paul, the prisoner of Jesus Christ for you Gentiles" (3: 1), "I therefore the prisoner of the Lord" (4: 1), "For which I am an ambassador in bonds" (6: 20)—that if Paul was the author of this letter—and there seems no sufficient reason for believing otherwise—it was in this period of custody in Rome that he wrote it; his period of imprisonment at Caesarea a little earlier has also been suggested, but Paul would have had less opportunity there. It was also while in custody in Rome that he wrote the similar letter to the Colossians (*Col.* 4: 10–11), his letter to his beloved Philippians (*Phil.* 1: 7, 4: 22), and his moving short appeal to Philemon on behalf of the runaway slave Onesimus (*Philem* 1: 9, 10, 23), which shows incidentally by the pun on the name—"in time past useless, but now useful (*onēsimos*) both to

---

[49] For the detailed argument see A. N. Sherwin-White, *op. cit.*, pp. 109-110.

you and to me" (*Philem* 1: 11)—that even in bonds Paul did not lose his sense of humour. From those letters we learn that he had as fellow-prisoners Aristarchus and Epaphras, that he brought Onesimus to acceptance of the Christian faith, and that there were Christians even in Nero's palace ("saints in Caesar's household") —no doubt among the slaves, for it was probably still true that "not many wise men after the flesh, not many mighty, not many noble are called" (*1 Cor.* 1: 26).

Acts ends with St. Paul in custody. The natural explanation is that he was still in custody when it was written, and it was written, as already maintained, as an *apologia*. Almost certainly Paul was brought to trial—the argument that he would be automatically released if his accusers did not appear within two years is not well founded. At that date it is unlikely that he would have been tried by Nero in person; it is more probable that at this date the trial was delegated, the Emperor merely reserving to himself confirmation of the sentence. It is also probable that Paul was acquitted. He himself expected such a result; he wrote to Philemon: "But withal prepare me also a lodging: for I trust that through your prayers I shall be given unto you" (*Philem* 1: 22).

Before we pass on to what followed Paul's acquittal, let us ask if there is any other detail about his missionary work so far that we can learn from other sources. Perhaps there is just one incident. It is generally thought that the *Acts of Paul and Thecla*, which is in part of the (generally worthless) *Acts of Paul* contains a substratum of truth. The story is that when Paul arrived at Iconium on his first missionary journey (*Acts* 13: 51) he lodged with Onesiphorus, and his preaching there on the virtue of chastity led Thecla to renounce Thamyris, to whom she was engaged. Thamyris took this amiss, Paul was charged before the civil authorities and beaten, while Thecla was condemned to death by burning but was miraculously saved. She died at Meriamlik, near Seleucia, where a large church was built over her supposed tomb. The tradition was enshrined not only in the Greek version but in five separate Latin translations as well as in Syriac, Armenian, Slavonic and Arabic. A tradition so strong probably has some foundation.

On the assumptions here made *Acts* could naturally have nothing to say about what followed Paul's acquittal. St. Clement, writing only about thirty years later,[50] says that he went to "the limits of the west", which suggests that he fulfilled his expressed desire to

---

[50] *Epistles* 1: 5, 7.

see Spain (*Rom.* 15: 24, 28). Cyril of Jerusalem, Epiphanius, Chrysostom and Jerome agree that he visited Spain, but if so the visit has not left any deep impression upon Spanish tradition.[51] It must be left an open question. Whether we can gain any further authentic information about Paul's travels at this time depends to some extent on our view of the letters to Timothy and Titus, the so-called Pastoral Epistles, as they presuppose a further period of missionary activity after release from captivity (*1 Tim.* 1: 17). Their authenticity has often been denied in modern times on stylistic grounds, but they all profess to be written by Paul, they are self-consistent and cohere with the genuine Pauline letters, and their differences in vocabulary are not such as to outweigh the universal consensus from Irenaeus and Tertullian in the second century that they are the work of Paul. Even sceptical critics generally allow that they incorporate genuine Pauline fragments. According to the evidence of the Pastoral Epistles Paul revisited Asia, Macedonia, Achaia and Crete. Paul asked Timothy to remain at Ephesus while he went to Macedonia (*1 Tim.* 1: 3); the subscription to the epistle says it was written from Laodicea. Paul left Titus in Crete,[52] and according to *Tit.* 1: 3 he had resolved to winter at Nicopolis in Macedonia; it was there, according to the subscription, that the letter was written.

The second epistle to Timothy presupposes that Paul was again a prisoner in Rome. Possibly he was arrested at Troas as he left his cloak there, and he asked Timothy to bring it to him along with "the books, but especially the parchments" (*2 Tim.* 4: 13) "The books" may have been mainly copies of the Old Testament scriptures but could have included Greek works. He had already made one appearance before the tribunal, and all men forsook him, but he was delivered out of the mouth of the lion (*2 Tim.* 4: 16–17). Only Luke was with him, and he asked for Mark, whom, it is pleasing to note, he again found "profitable to us for the ministry" (*2 Tim.* 4: 11). A famous name, Linus, perhaps that of an early Bishop of Rome, as already suggested, appears among Paul's companions who send greetings (*2 Tim.* 4: 21). There is a reference to Erastus whom he had left at Corinth and to Trophimus

---

[51] Among the apostles it is St James who is specially venerated in Spain, but the tradition that he visited Spain can hardly be reconciled with *Acts*, which implies that the apostles did not leave Jerusalem until after his death.

[52] The theory sometimes advanced that Paul dropped Titus at Fair Havens in Crete on his voyage to Rome—and wrote the *Epistle to Titus* in his first (and only) period of captivity in the capital is not really tenable. Paul was an exceptional prisoner, and may have had exceptional privileges, but he would hardly be allowed to establish bishoprics as a captive.

—the immediate cause of the attempted lynching in Jerusalem—whom he had left at Miletus.

On this occasion Paul did not expect acquittal. "I am now ready to be offered", he wrote, "and the time of my departure is at hand" (2 *Tim.* 4: 6). The first of the Roman persecutions of Christians had been set in motion by Nero in 64 when he made them scapegoats for the great fire of that year, and the atmosphere was now quite different from what it had been at the time of Paul's earlier trial. (The favourable picture of Roman rule given in *Acts* would hardly have been drawn at any time after this date; if *Acts* had been composed at a later date, its view of Roman rule is more likely to have resembled that in the Apocalypse, probably composed during Domitian's persecution.) According to Eusebius Paul suffered martyrdom in 67, and Tertullian [53] adds the detail that he was beheaded by the sword, which was a Roman citizen's right. *The Acts of St. Paul* gives the scene of his martyrdom as a place on the left bank of the Tiber about three miles from Rome. His body was taken to a cemetery nearer Rome, lying just off the road to Ostia and belonging to a Christian matron, Lucina. Although removed out of fear of desecration during the Valerian persecution it was brought back, and over it Constantine erected the great basilica later known as San Paolo fuori le mura. Though his headless body lay beneath a few feet of Italian soil, his work had been so well done that it proved indestructible and has, indeed, endured to this day.

FOR FURTHER READING

W. M. Ramsay (Sir William Ramsay):
  The Church in the Roman Empire before A.D. 170 (London, 1893, 7th ed., 1903).
  St. Paul the Traveller and Roman Citizen (London, 1895. 18th ed., 1935).
  The Cities of St. Paul: their influence on his life and thought (London, 1907).

H. V. Morton: *In the steps of St. Paul* (London, 1936).
Malcolm Muggeridge and Alec Vidler: *Paul, Envoy Extraordinary* (London, 1972).
Stewart Perowne: *The Journeys of St. Paul* (London, 1973).

[53] *De praescriptionibus adversus haereticos*, 36, *Patrologia Latina*, J. P. Migne ed., Vol. 2, p. 49.

Roland Allen, *Missionary Methods: St. Paul's or Ours?* (London, 1912, new ed., 1960).

Ernst Haenchen: *The Acts of the Apostles: A Commentary*, translated from the 14th German edition (London, 1971).

Günther Bornkamm: *Paul,* translated from *Paulus* (Stuttgart, 1969) by D. M. G. Stalker (London, 1971).

A. N. Sherwin-White, *Roman Society and Roman Law in the New Testament* (Oxford, 1963, new edition, 1969).

Other references will be found in the footnotes to the text.

CHAPTER V

ST. PAUL'S SHIPWRECK

by

Angus Acworth

BEFORE getting down to the detailed argument about the place of St. Paul's shipwreck I would like to make two preliminary points. First, although it must have been a harrowing experience, the shipwreck was an unimportant incident in St. Paul's life: it was quite without effect on his mission. Whether he was wrecked on this island or that is of no religious significance. My concern, as a lawyer and historian, is to ascertain the truth in regard to what has been called the most famous shipwreck in history.

Secondly, in submitting to you as I shall that the shipwreck took place on the Dalmatian island now called Mljet, I am not putting forward any novel theory. The shipwreck took place on the island of Melita (Greek, *Melite*[1]) but since both Malta and Mljet were called Melita in Roman times, there is necessarily ambiguity. In his survey of the Byzantine Empire *De Imperii Administratione* the Emperor Constantine Porphyrogenitus, who reigned in the 10th century, that is, a thousand years ago named Mljet as the place of the shipwreck. And he, of course, had no axe to grind. The claim by Malta came later. In 1523 the Knights of St. John were ousted from Rhodes by the Turks. They spent a rather uneasy seven years in Rome—there was not really room in the Renaissance city for *both* the Supreme Pontiff *and* the Grand Master of a Sovereign Order. Then in 1530 the Holy Roman Emperor Charles V ceded Malta to the Knights. They were a wealthy international religious order drawn from the aristocracies of western Europe—there were eight *langues*—who would have a particular interest in St. Paul, the Apostle to the Gentiles; and they would willingly assume that the Melita on which St. Paul's ship was

---

[1] The better reading is *Melitene*. The suffix *-ne* is, according to the philologists, "adjectival". But one does not talk of landing in French or touching down in Roman. It appears from Ptolemy's *Geography*, written a century after the shipwreck, that though both Malta and Mljet were officially called *Melite*, Mljet was commonly known as *Melitene*, possibly a popular abbreviation of *Melite nēsos*, Melite Island.

wrecked was *their* island. The church dedicated to St. Paul in what is now called St. Paul's Bay dates from the end of the 16th century, that is to say, it was built about sixty years after the Knights went into residence. In the eighteenth and nineteenth centuries there was a considerable literature on the subject, some arguing this way, others arguing that way. The case for Malta is, however, generally considered to have been established by James Smith in his book *Voyage and Shipwreck of St. Paul*. This, however, was published in 1848. I do not need to tell you that there have since then been considerable advances in historical methodology, cartography, meteorology and oceanography. It seemed to me to be about time someone took a new look at the matter. My qualifications, other than those of a lawyer and historian, are that—apparently alone of the commentators—I have visited *both* Malta *and* Mljet (to my mind a necessary exercise); I also know something about sailing.

The only contemporary account of the shipwreck is contained in the last two chapters of the *Acts of the Apostles* written in Greek by St. Luke. He was an educated man, the colleague and companion of St. Paul, an on-the-spot witness of what he describes. His account can properly be regarded as trustworthy.

That being said, let me sketch in the background though you will know it well enough. The Jews were thirsting for St. Paul's blood but Festus, the Roman Governor at Caesarea, after hearing the accusations felt reluctant to deal with the case and proposed to send St. Paul to Jerusalem for trial. St. Paul, however, in exercise of his rights as a Roman citizen, appealed to Caesar. It seems probable that the Apostle was anxious to make his way to the capital of the Roman world and this was an opportunity of going there at public expense, albeit as a prisoner. There were, of course, no regular sailings in those days and Julius, the centurion who had charge of St. Paul and other prisoners, had to make such arrangements as he could. In due course, the party boarded a vessel which took them to Sidon, in what is now Lebanon, and then, by way of the north of Cyprus, to Myra (now called Demre) on the south coast of Asia Minor. There the party transhipped and boarded an Alexandrian vessel bound for Italy. This set off on a south-west course, passed Salmone, at the east end of Crete and put in at Fair Havens on the south coast. As the season was far advanced—it was probably mid-October, and mid-October to mid-February was a close season for navigation on the high seas—St. Paul urged the centurion to winter there. But the captain wanted to move to a better harbour some forty miles farther west at Phoinika (now called Foinikias). Julius naturally supported the captain. The ship set sail with a fair wind on the port beam; but before long the wind veered from south to south-east and a storm sprang up. The ship had to run before it and after being buffeted for fourteen days was finally wrecked on Melita. In the spring another ship the *Castor and Pollux,* which had been wintering in Melita, took St. Paul and rest first to Syracuse, where they spent three days, then to Reggio in the Straits of Messina and so to Pozzuoli in the Bay of Naples (it is now half-submerged and out of business). The remainder of the journey was made by road—the Via Appia Antica.

The crucial part of the voyage is, of course, the two legs Fair Havens-Melita and Melita-Syracuse. Fair Havens, despite its name, is not a place a ship's captain would choose to winter in. It is a roadstead open to the south-east—and the Meteorological Office has informed me that south-easterly gales are common in this part of the Mediterranean in the winter months; in a Force 8 wind anchors might have dragged and the ship driven ashore. And so the captain wanted to move some forty miles west to Phoinika for greater safety. The current (1962) Admiralty chart shows it

THE HARBOUR OF PHENICE (PHOINIKA)
as shown in the French Admiralty Chart of 1738
Ref.: James Smith, *Voyage and Shipwreck of St. Paul* (1848), p. 50, Malta Library

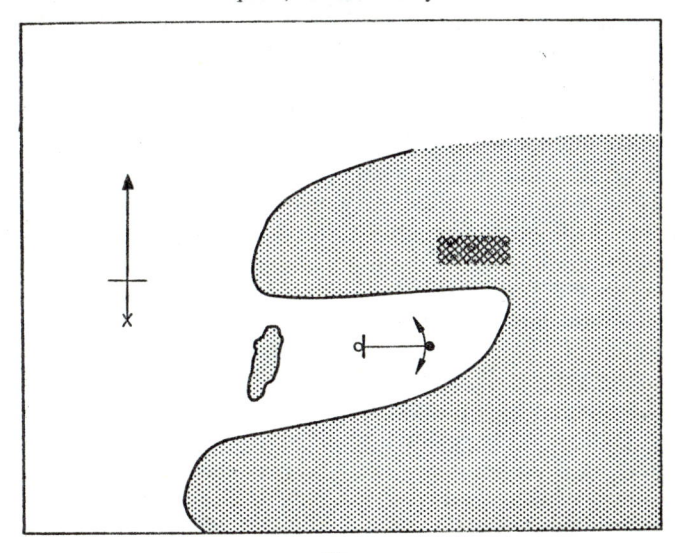

F

facing west so that it is not exposed to south-easterly gales and it has its anchorage. But the sea bed is constantly changing and it does not answer to St. Luke's description since there is no sandbank (*syrtis*) acting as a mole and separating the two entrances which he tells us looked 30° south and 30° north of west. There is however (inset) a French Admiralty chart which shows Phoinika as it was in 1738. You will see that it corresponds exactly with St. Luke's description and also that if the ship had been able to make it, she could have lain at anchor comfortably through the winter. And so it was decided to make the move.

The ship started off with a moderate south wind, that is, on the port beam. After rounding Cape Lukinos and changing course to north-west, the wind would be on the port quarter and if it had continued there would have been no difficulty in making harbour. But not long after rounding the Cape, the wind veered to south-east and increased to gale strength. Any of you who have gone in for sailing will realize that it would have been very dangerous to try to enter the harbour of Phoinika since the ship would almost certainly have been driven on to the sandbank which protected it. It is also a rule when a vessel is caught in a storm to stand clear of the lee shore. And so the captain stood to sea. Under the lee of the island of Cauda he lowered the yard which carried the mainsail, got in the boat and undergirt the ship. Then with only a stormsail set, he ran before the wind. A glance at a map of the central Mediterranean shows that a south-east gale would have driven the ship into the Adriatic; and in fact St. Luke tells us that the ship was carried into Adria, the Greek and also the Latin word for the Adriatic. After fourteen days when they were in effect sailing blind, they found land ahead but, failing to make the entrance to an inlet, ran aground on its western shore. Although the ship was broken up, all the ship's complement got safely to land. If you look at a map of the south Adriatic, you will see that Mljet, the southernmost of the Dalmatian islands, would have lain across the path of a ship driving north-west; and at its western end there is an inlet or creek (I have been there) which would have afforded good and sheltered anchorage to the *Castor and Pollux,* the ship which took the party to Syracuse and Pozzuoli in the spring.

If the wind which caught the ship was south-east, James Smith as a yachtsman recognized that shipwreck on Malta was not possible. And so he argues that the wind was in fact Euraquilon, a reading which occurs in a number of the codices, and not Euroclydon (this only calls for a two letter change in Greek).

Euraquilon, a word which does not appear anywhere else in Greek literature, is in fact a hybrid, a curious combination of Euros, the Greek south-east wind, and Aquilon, the Latin north wind. The dictionary construes this as a "north-easter". But a north-east wind, equally with a south-east one, would not have carried the ship to Malta. And so James Smith splits the difference, treats it as an east-north-east wind which he argues would, allowing for leeway, have taken the ship in a direct line to Malta. Apart from philological difficulties, there are two substantial objections to Smith's contention. First, St. Luke states specifically that the wind blew *against*, that is in the direction of, the shore; secondly, if the wind was north-east or east-north-east, that is off-shore, there would have been no danger of running aground on the sandbank.

Let us now return to Mljet. Despite the break-up of the ship all its complement got safely to land and, so we are told, found that the island was called Melita. James Smith admits that it is surprising that an Alexandrian crew should not have immediately recognized Malta, a well-known port of call. Surprising indeed: but there would be no reason for them to recognize Mljet which was off the beaten track. Stewart Perowne in his recent book on the *Journeys of St. Paul* has also made the comment that the islanders would appear from St. Luke's account to be "uncouth peasants" (which would probably be an apt enough description of the inhabitants of Mljet) whereas the Maltese were sophisticated and skilled artisans and craftsmen with an export trade in semi-luxury textile and metal goods.

Once ashore—and they had to swim for it—they lit a fire to dry themselves. Adders, venomous snakes whose bites can kill, are known to be attracted by fire; and in the event an adder fastened itself on St. Paul's arm. But, before it had time to bite, he shook it off into the fire. Today there are no poisonous snakes in either Malta or Mljet. There never have been adders in Malta; on the other hand, until the beginning of the present century, Mljet was infested with them. Then someone, taking his cue from Kipling's *Jungle Book*, imported two pairs of mongooses from India. Their favourite diet is rats and snakes, and they cleared the island. If St. Paul was wrecked on Mljet, the episode of the snake makes sense; if on Malta, where did the reptile come from?

There are two or three more points I might make, all tending the same way; but enough is enough. To summarize: (1) a south-east gale would have driven the ship into the Adriatic; (2) St. Luke confirms that the ship was tossed about in Adria, the Greek and also the Latin name for the Adriatic; (3) a ship beating north-west in the Adriatic would find Mljet lying across its path; (4) the Alexandrian crew did not recognize the island although they would have been familiar with Malta; (5) the islanders were simple peasants whereas the Maltese were sophisticated artisans and craftsmen; (6) St. Paul was attacked by an adder—but there never have been adders in Malta.

I will adduce only one more historic fact, though it is persuasive rather than compelling evidence. In October, 1192 (the same time of the year you will note) Richard Coeur-de-Lion set sail from Palestine at the end of the Fourth Crusade. His ship was wrecked on Lokrum. And where, you may ask, is Lokrum? It is a small island, close to the shore, near Dubrovnik, some twenty miles east and a little to the south of Mljet. St. Paul was not the only VIP to be wrecked on a Dalmatian island.

Those then are the relevant facts and matters. My submission to you is that the Emperor Constantine Porphyrogenitus was quite right in naming Mljet as the place of the shipwreck.

CHAPTER 6

ST. PAUL THE WRITER

by
C. J. A. Hickling

THE style is the man; and never more so than with Paul. And the man, in Paul above all, is the whole man, "called as an Apostle, separated out for the Gospel of God" (*Rom.* 1: 1): we cannot think of Paul having a private life. To consider Paul the writer, then, is to consider Paul the apostle, doing his work as an apostle to so remarkable an extent by correspondence (cf. *2 Cor.* 10: 10!); it is to consider him as the Christian thinker and teacher who, perhaps more than any of his successors, transformed the course of history by his continual rapid dictation of letters. As good a starting-point as any for this essay, then, will be to reflect for a few minutes how things would have been had he not been the writer he was; to try, at least, to appreciate the size of the gap that would be left—in more senses than one—if as we turned the pages of our New Testaments we went straight from the last page of *Acts* to the beginning of *Hebrews* (almost universally agreed now to be from another hand than Paul's). It is some testimony to the place Paul's letters have in our consciousness—as Christians, as Western Europeans, in a sense as Anglo-Saxons, so deeply has the Bible affected our cultural identity—that this is an imaginative feat that is almost impossible for us. Nevertheless, the exercise will be instructive.

Scholarly opinion, then (so we can imagine a lecturer beginning an account of Christian origins in the circumstances we are imagining) has for long noted the remarkable role attributed to Paul in the early consolidation and expansion of Christianity. Conservative researchers, ascribing a high historical value to *Acts* taken at face value, have always regarded this man as the pioneer of the Christian mission throughout the civilized world. Luke, who (they claim) knew what he was talking about, describes no other missionary working outside Israel except for a few men who were Paul's companions. Scholarship of a less conservative bias is of course less confident that this is the whole picture.

There might have been good reasons, partly or wholly concealed from us now, why the author of *Luke-Acts* should have regarded this mysterious figure so highly. But the portrait, on either view, certainly suggests that some historical figure lies behind it. Here is a man who is presented as a brilliant missionary preacher, eloquent, versatile, an indefatigable traveller, the founder of a whole series of churches, and moreover a man with remarkable miraculous powers. Naturally—so the second type of scholar would add—much of this portrait is legendary. But there was a real personality behind the legend. What would we give to have more information about a man who would so soon give rise to such a legend as this!

German scholarship (our lecturer continues) had for some time drawn attention to a further significant element in the problem of this figure called Paul. The second Epistle of Peter refers, in a much debated passage (3: 15f), to men who have tried to prove the truth of their heretical contentions by misapplying the teaching of "Paul" as it might be found in some letters he was clearly held to have composed. Making use of their well-known intuitive insight, these students of the matter had not been slow to deduce that the man behind the Pauline legend had enjoyed a certain reputation in the Church of the second century (or at least in some of the local churches of that century) as the author of influential documents. What would we not give, they went on, for even a small fragment of the genuine writings of this man! The writer of *2 Peter* seems to regard "Paul's" writings as being on a par with the inspired scriptures of the Old Testament: a very striking and indeed astonishing claim for someone who had died —presumably—only some decades ago. *Acts* cannot have been far wrong in its estimate of this man's importance in the very earliest Church History.

Some of the more radical scholars went further still. No smoke without fire, they said. If the orthodox writer of *2 Peter* can claim that the heretics made use of writings attributed to this "Paul", was there not perhaps in those lost letters something which gave some colour to the allegation? Should we discover that the genuine Paul of history—for all that *Acts* say about him—was in fact more than a little of a gnostic himself: that the doctrines of the hidden wisdom and of the rescue of the elect from mankind's fatal enmeshment with matter, adjudged heretical by the Great Church, might prove to have been present in the writings of the real Paul? Increasingly (in the fable we are devising) the world of New Testament scholarship looked eagerly for the possibility that, in the library of some ancient monastery in Egypt or Sinai, someone would come across a few fragments of a genuine letter of Paul.

We can add (our speaker proceeds) a further reason for their eagerness. The discussion—which had of course been vigorous at an early stage in New Testament studies—whether there had ever been a historical Paul at all had been virtually brought to an end when the famous Gallio inscription had been found. This stone inscription (which was first published in a Russian series of 1894-5) must refer to the Gallio of *Acts* 18: 12, and by its rather precise—if not indeed quite unambiguous—dating it enables us to fix the date of Paul's arrival in Corinth, described in *Acts* 18: 1, as having taken place in AD 51 or 52.[1] On this evidence, Paul was working in Corinth only some twenty years after the Crucifixion! If, then, it was observed, letters should turn up written not long after that date, even perhaps letters relating to Paul's evangelism in Corinth itself, we should have first-hand evidence of incomparably precious value for the nature of the very earliest form of Christianity. All students of the subject (our imaginary scholar went on) would of course have agreed that such a Christianity would be simple and undeveloped, with no dogmas such as that of the Resurrection or the belief that Jesus had an existence before he appeared on earth. It would no doubt prove to be a Christianity without creeds or sacraments. Nevertheless, how splendid it would be to find light thrown on this vital first stage of Christian history. But of course, these students reminded themselves with a sigh, such a hope was idle, and research must proceed largely in the dark with such evidence as was available.

Such, let us suppose, was the situation in 1931 as portrayed by the lecturer of our fable. Imagine, then, the headlines in the papers when in that year (here we return to fact) some Egyptian peasants discovered a small pamphlet made of papyrus leaves and in quite good condition, containing no fewer than eight letters of varying length which claimed in their opening verses to have been written by a certain Paul, who could surely be none other than the mysterious Paul of *Acts!* Imagine the further shock of amazement throughout the scholarly world and indeed throughout Christendom when it was understood that two of the letters in this collection (which we know as Papyrus 46) were addressed to no other city but Corinth itself—the very place where we know Paul to have been working as early as AD 51 or 52! Within hours

---

[1] A translation of the inscription is given, with a concise note on its chronological significance, in *The New Testament Background: Selected Documents*, by C. K. Barrett (London, 1961), pp. 48f.

of their discovery the letters had been read, for they are written in a very clear hand in Greek; moreover, experts in handwriting dated them to within a few years either way of AD 200. Classical students were astonished to the point of incredulity. A classical manuscript dating not much more than a century and a half from the date at which the original autograph had been composed! Unheard-of, altogether extraordinary. There would be priceless evidence available now of the Greek of everyday life in the Empire during the first century AD.

We may continue the fantasy for one final stage and still find that it makes useful points. The Vatican, of course, was at first alarmed. What would Protestant scholars say about the ecclesiastical dogmas of the Trinity, the Church, the Sacraments, now surely to be exposed beyond doubt as chilly perversions of the early simplicities? Dominican and Jesuit libraries had never been so full of learned Fathers preparing their answers. But what was the astonishment of the liberal German researchers themselves as they studied the newly-found *1 Corinthians* to find that there was a Eucharist regularly celebrated at Corinth, with a ritual recalling the Last Supper and indeed with a description of that Supper itself some twenty years earlier than the oldest one known up to that point! Moreover, a doctrine of something like the Real Presence was clearly taken for granted. People were baptized; the Church was viewed as nothing less than the Body of Christ. Jesus was regularly called "Lord"—a title suggesting divinity—and coupled with the Father as a participant in the creation of the Universe (8: 6). The whole history of Christian doctrine would have to be rewritten. All the characteristic tenets of catholic Christianity had become common coin within the first twenty years of the Church's existence; and this was henceforth to be recognized, not on the basis of conjecture, but of solid evidence.

Other voices, however—and here we return more directly to the subject of "Paul the Writer"—were soon to be heard commenting on this astonishing find. "Let us at once rescue these priceless documents from the hands of the New Testament experts", they cried. "These people are well known to be drudges, not all that harmless, either, who lack imagination and have no sense for what is noble and beautiful in literature. For these letters are a unique monument to the human spirit! They are the literary achievement of a genius! What superb command of Greek! What magnificent flexibility of style! Almost unbelievable that one man can rise to the rhetorical height of *1 Cor.* 13 and *Rom.* 8, and yet reproduce on paper the authentic sound of passionate personal argument as in *Gal.* 3. What a writer! These letters", they pronounced, "must at once find their place among the world's classics as examples of the passionate religious self-awareness of a highly complex, but above all brilliantly articulate intellect who towers above most writers of his own period and ranks pretty high among all others". Historians took up the cry. "Here", they said, "is the first modern man. We had known self-awareness, self-analysis, self-disclosure before now in the cultural history of this period and preceding ones. But it was sophisticated, artificial, a pose for the benefit of a public, and never without a trace of gaucheness. Here is one whose self-awareness is no literary convention, but is deeply sincere, yet at the same time something he is able to communicate to the rest of us for his own urgent purposes."

This little exercise in rewriting history has been intended to serve several purposes. The imaginary loss of Paul's letters at an early period serves as a reminder how enormously valuable they are for their literary and cultural worth, and for their contribution to the reconstruction of Christian theological history. The attempt has also been made, in this fable, to indicate how sketchy—or at best, how controversial—are the available indications of the historical and theological framework in which we have to try to place Paul (or in which we do place him, with often inadequate attention to the many uncertainties involved[2]). Sketchy, indeed, these indications remain. Even the chronology of the letters themselves is disputable, and still keenly disputed, in some cases. A majority of scholars would agree in seeing the Corinthian correspondence and *Romans* as forming the amazing achievement—in terms of the thought behind them—of three or four years in the early to middle fifties of the first century. Some would wish to place *Galatians* and *Philippians* within the same very short period; but there is still a strong case for the older and conservative view that *Galatians* is earlier than *1 Thessalonians* (which is by common consent to be dated about AD 51-2), and that *Philippians* was written from Paul's captivity in Rome in 58–60, not from an earlier period of imprisonment in Ephesus or elsewhere. *Ephesians* is regarded by many, and *2 Thessalonians* and *Colossians* by some,

[2] I have tried to discuss some of these uncertainties in "On Putting Paul in his Place", in *What about the New Testament?* (Essays in honour of C. F. Evans), edited by M. D. Hooker and C. J. A. Hickling (London, 1975), pp. 76-88.

as by other hands than Paul's. Equally important for evaluating Paul is the view that we should take of *Acts:* if it is a late work, making use of only fragmentary data about Paul, its use as a basis for a biography of Paul, and hence as providing contexts for his letters, becomes very limited.[3]

We commonly take too much for granted, then, in the historical groundwork for our assessment of Paul. But above all—and this has been the main purpose of the above flight of fancy—we take Paul himself too much for granted. We do so, to a great extent, precisely because he is "in the Bible". Yet it is far from clear how he comes to be there at all. Most of his letters were written to deal with problems of short duration, or so at any rate he hoped! Paul must be astonished—as St. Matthew or St. Luke, we may suppose, are not, in the case of their own more deliberate contributions to the collection of sacred writings—to find himself being read in church twenty centuries later. No doubt an individual or group with a particularly strong devotion to Paul's memory collected his letters and gave them a wider circulation; though we may well guess that their intrinsic depth and vigour assisted the process of their inclusion in the Church's new holy book. At all events, there is food for thought in the reflection that one man's responses to situations which were largely local and very short-term should have achieved a place in what has become our Bible —even though that place, because the Bible is a "religious book", has masked from us much of the sharp focus and brilliant colour of Paul's writings themselves.

Let us try, then, in our approach to Paul the writer, to grasp the sheer stature of the man, in all but the physical sense (if there is any truth in the apocryphal writing which describes him as short[4]). John Donne said "Wheresoever I open St. Paul's epistles, I meet not words but thunder, and universal thunder, thunder that passes through the world". Some more recent judgments are no less impressive. "It would be no great loss to exchange the theological literature of a whole generation of later epochs against a single Epistle of St. Paul." "In the whole range of literature there

---

[3] For a brief discussion of the problems of Pauline chronology, see the article "The Chronology of the New Testament" by G. Ogg in *Peake's Commentary on the Bible*, edited by M. Black and H. H. Rowley (London, 1963). A good general introduction to the study of the Pauline letters is *St. Paul and his Letters*, by F. W. Beare (London, 1962).

[4] That is, the late second-century *Acts of Paul and Thecla*, 3 (translation in *The New Testament Apocrypha*, by F. Hennecke, edited by W. Schneemelcher, translated by R. McL. Wilson, Vol. 2, London, 1965).

is nothing like St. Paul's letters. Other correspondence may be more voluminous, more elaborate, more studiously demonstrative. But none is so faithful a mirror of the writer." "Paul, what a man he must have been! "[5]

As we have seen, Paul the man—Paul the human individual—cannot be separated from Paul the writer, and neither can be seen apart from Paul the theologian. Although, therefore, his achievement as a theologian is the subject of other essays in this volume, some trespassing must be allowed. You cannot study a man who is a genius in the potency of his self-expression without asking both what it is that he strives so vehemently to express, and also what is the driving force of conviction that leads him to say what he does with such peculiar intensity. There is a one-word answer to both these questions: the Gospel. Here was a man knowing himself to be charged (possibly believing that no one else held or ever could hold this charge on an equal footing with himself[6]) to bring the triumphant statement of God's final act of rescue to the entire non-Jewish world. Much of the quality of Paul's writing springs from this underlying sense of urgency and privilege. There was no one else to say what he must say. No wonder he said it so well.

In considering the content of Paul's gospel in slightly closer detail, we shall therefore already be noting, and accounting for, some of the outstanding features of his writing. It was a gospel for all men; and yet it always remained, for him, essentially the gospel for Israel. In this two-sidedness—which at some points, we may suspect, Paul does not altogether harmonize—lies one of the clues to the extraordinary multiplicity of styles which is characteristic of him, "Lively, rough, polished, sly, sarcastic, then all at once tender, delicate, almost roguish and coaxing", he is "skilful in interspersing his style with moments of reticence and reserve, ... with unkind allusions, with affected ironies": such is the comment of a critic who himself shares some, at least, of these

---

[5] The last three quotations are respectively from the writings of Leo Chestov, Bishop J. B. Lightfoot and Karl Barth, and all four are taken from the fascinating collection of testimonies assembled by Malcolm Muggeridge and A. R. Vidler in *Paul: Envoy Extraordinary* (London, 1972), pp. 11-16.

[6] The possibility that Paul held this view is discussed in "On Putting Paul in his Place", see note 2.

qualities.[7] To some extent, this capacity for variety is linked with the many levels of his perception of what God was doing and of what men were failing to do.

Thus, Paul was willing to be "all things to all men" (*1 Cor.* 9: 22) in the service of a gospel which was for all mankind. To the Greeks he was as a Greek, and a knowledgeable and sensitive one at that, as befitted an educated "citizen of no mean city" (which was, of course, Tarsus, *Acts* 21: 39). There is an element of Stoic thinking which lends its own peculiar dignity to some of Paul's writing; at some points, interestingly enough, blending with strands that emerge from the thought-world of the immediate circle of Jesus. Thus in *Philippians* 4: 11–13 we have a balanced and economical statement of the contentment, almost the resignation, the detachment from things earthly, of the Stoic sage. The brief parallels of opposites—"I know how to be humbled, I know also how to be affluent; in every respect and in all ways I have been initiated into the secret of being satiated and of starving, of experiencing both superfluous abundance and want"—move calmly to their climax: "I am ready for anything in him who empowers me", the sentence which indeed the Stoic would have found it harder to write than he would what went before. Yet behind this passage the warning of Jesus in *Matthew* 6: 25ff. against anxiety is not very far away. Less plainly, Paul's discussion of marriage and the single life in *1 Cor.* 7—even though the thought of the impending end of the world is the leading consideration—has clear undertones of Stoic liberation from distraction, as some of the wording brings out[8]; and vv. 29–31, for example (which are not dissimilar from the passage in *Philippians* which we have just considered) build up a climax which is measured and unhurried. Elsewhere, too, we find from time to time the tone of reasonable persuasiveness bravely and not unsuccessfully attempted by one to whom, we may fairly say, sweet reasonableness did not come easily.

---

[7] E. Renan, *St. Paul*, p. 232, quoted by Robert Sencourt, *Saint Paul: Envoy of Grace* (London, 1948), p. 234. Renan's description of Paul, quoted by Muggeridge and Vidler (see note 5) is striking: "What sort of man was Paul? Not by any means a saint. Goodness was far from being his most notable characteristic. He was proud, unbending, imperious; he was self-assertive and masterful; he used hard words; he believed that he was absolutely right; he stuck to his opinions; he quarrelled with many people."

[8] This point is made by Hans Conzelmann in his great commentary on *1 Corinthians* translated by J. W. Leitch (Philadelphia, 1975).

Yet "to the Jews" Paul "became as a Jew"; and he could write in *Galatians* as only a Jew could have done to men who were not Jews but who were anxious to take every necessary step in order to count as "Abraham's offspring" (*Gal.* 3: 29). This is why Paul's prose is sometimes rendered complex and even tortuous by a style of argument characteristic of Jewish exposition, which hops, in what we must admit to be a somewhat ungainly way, from one stepping-stone in the Old Testament to another, and is often in danger of slipping off altogether when some of these stepping-stones do not seem to bear the weight that is being put upon them. Indeed, it must be conceded that controversy—in which Paul is engaged in the exegetical arguments in question—does not always lend itself to fine writing; and Paul was a controversialist to the core. But the passion of his conviction drives him on; and one can at least say of passages like *Gal.* 3 and 4 and *Rom.* 9–11 that he somehow conveys a sense of the beauty and coherence of God's purpose for the baptized that is in fundamental contrast with the ultimate triviality of the alternative ways of salvation canvassed by his opponents. The conflict between beauty and triviality makes itself felt as you follow the argument through. And afterwards Paul has a way of emerging breathless from a tunnel of technical exegesis of the Old Testament—such as would have charmed the rabbis as much as its conclusions exasperated them— and coming out into a "level place" where his style suddenly expands into those limpidly simple, broad, joyfully confident affirmations which are perhaps his best writing: *Gal.* 3: 26–9 and *Rom.* 11: 28–32 (with the famous "O altitudo" doxology leading out from it)—each of them following a long passage of close reasoning from texts in the rabbinical style—are good examples.

It is ironic, then, though certainly not without foundation, that Paul's writing should have a common reputation for obscurity. For he is above all, in the recently current jargon, a communicator; and, as with some other communicators of Christian truth, occasional failure to make his meaning clear in detail, to people who can have so little idea what the situations he wrote for were really like, only slightly qualifies his splendid success in communicating his own deep conviction. It is a success which in large measure lies in his capacity to realize the sense of personal address in all that he writes. The tone of the spoken word, uttered to rebuke, correct, persuade or move particular individuals with whom we can identify ourselves, characterizes all the variations of style and mood we have been considering. A recent writer on the rhetoric of the New Testament—and rhetoric, in its true sense, is the art of persuasion—has said:

"Paul wrote reluctantly and . . . always as one thwarted by absence and eagerly anticipating meeting or reunion. He is distressed by circumstances which prevent face-to-face address. . . . Even in writing he falls into the style of direct oral plea and challenge. The very nature of the Gospel imposes upon him ways of expression that suggest dramatic immediacy: devices and rhythms of the speaker rather than the writer; imagined dialogue; the situation of a court hearing or church trial with its accusations and defences; the use of direct discourse; challenges not so much to understand the written words but to listen and behold; queries, exclamations and oaths." [9]

Always we hear Paul's voice behind the written Greek; and in trying to set out the qualities that make him so great a writer, we should perhaps give some place to the truly impressive achievement of Tertius (*Rom.* 16: 22) and Paul's other secretaries, who somehow captured with their not altogether sophisticated stenography[10] the authentic flow of dictation that must have often been intolerably rapid. So we may conclude by turning to two passages, varying greatly in the level of their subject-matter, in which this sense of immediacy underlies, as it always does, a fairly high degree of complexity of thought and expression.

First, the little note to Philemon. Since the discoveries of so many fragments of personal correspondence among the papyrus finds in Egypt, we now have material with which to compare this note, which is a letter of commendation written to the owner of the runaway slave Onesimus; for Paul had not only converted him but had also—perhaps with somewhat scant regard for the law—retained him in his imprisonment as personal assistant. The comparison between *Philemon* and contemporary personal letters can easily be made, for the texts and translations of the latter are

---

[9] Amos N. Wilder, *Early Christian Rhetoric* (The New Testament Library: London, 1964), pp. 22f.

[10] A system of shorthand known as tachygraphy is known to have been in use from at least the second century AD onwards (*Oxford Classical Dictionary*, 2nd ed., 1970, *s.v.* "tachygraphy"). It is difficult, however, to think that this somewhat cumbrous system helped Tertius and his colleagues very much.

readily accessible.[11] Even allowing for the fact that none of them has to deal with a state of affairs as delicate and even potentially embarrassing as is the case in *Philemon*, Paul's plea to his friend has a spontaneous vital flow, and yet also a touch of slightly mannered sophistication (as in the play on the meaning of Onesimus' name—"useful"—" . . . who was once useless but is now useful, both to you and to me", v. 11), which have no parallel at all in the papyrus letters.

The second passage is, in the best and fullest sense, far more rhetorical; and it is worth noting that, even if not by contemporary standards—which were exacting—precisely a trained rhetorician, Paul could write "passages which both by style and content belong to [his] struggle with rhetorically trained opponents for the support of his rhetorically fastidious converts".[12] These passages, however, are those in which Paul engages with, while at the same time profoundly criticizing, the contemporary rhetorical convention of concern with one's own reputation. We must look elsewhere for the great heights of rhetoric in a wider sense. *1 Cor.* 13 is sufficiently well known to speak for itself; though we may note that close study reveals the extraordinarily complex debt of this chapter both to Greek and to Jewish traditions of style and of teaching alike, to such an extent that some have thought that this great hymn, standing as it does rather aside from its context in the letter, may have been taken as a whole by Paul from some other source.[13] Instead, let us briefly analyse the climax of the greatest chapter in *Romans*, itself surely the greatest of all Paul's writings. The verses in question are *Rom.* 8: 31–9.[14]

First, we notice the combination of structural formality with a looseness making for rapid forward movement in vv. 31–6. Paul builds up his climax of statements concerning God's boundless love for us by means of a sequence of rhetorical questions, with their answers interwoven with them (vv. 32a, 33b, 34). His assertion of Christ's love is made clearly in the last of these questions,

---

[11] In *Light from the Ancient East*, by Adolf Deissmann (London, 1910), especially chapter 3.

[12] This description is taken from a valuable article on rhetorical forms and conventions in Paul by a classical scholar, Edwin Judge: 'Paul's Boasting in Relation to Contemporary Professional Practice', Australian Biblical Review, 16 (1968), p. 48.

[13] See H. Conzelmann's commentary on this passage (as in note 8).

[14] These verses were declaimed in Greek as the conclusion of the talk to the Advanced Sunday School at St. Andrew-by-the-Wardrobe which formed the basis of the present contribution.

v. 35, and then the accelerating list of afflictions leads on to a brief pause in the quotation of *Psalm* 44, with the further rounding-off of what had gone before in v. 37. And then Paul really "takes off", and the series of nouns in vv. 38f—echoing the list in v. 35, but now a scale which is not less than cosmic—finally emerges into the triumphant, calm, and magnificent assertion contained in the last phrases of the whole passage. Dynamic rhythms alternate with the balanced antithesis of vv. 31–34; statements made in the form of a negative highlight the simplicity of "did not spare his Son" and "in all these things we do far more than conquer". No wonder this has remained one of the classic utterances of the faith of a Christian.

"His presence as a man", said Paul's critics in a passage to which we have already alluded (*2 Cor.* 10: 10), "is unimpressive and indeed beneath contempt, but his letters are powerful and weighty". It is a testimony with which no one can disagree. Paul possessed in superlative measure the power of the pen, which is the power to persuade and to move. In his case, it is the power of a man's own hold on a faith to which he is most deeply committed married to his urgent concern for particular people he loves. Paul the writer is Paul the theologian, but even more he is Paul the pastor, the shepherd who "gives his soul" (if we translate *John* 10: 11 literally) "on behalf of the sheep".

CHAPTER 7

ST. PAUL ON GRACE

by
Gordon Huelin

"ALL is of Grace and Grace is for all." With those words Dr. James Moffatt introduced the section of his book *Grace in the New Testament*, published in 1931, in which he dealt with St. Paul's teaching on Grace,[1] still, as far as I am aware, the fullest treatment of the subject in the English language and covering nearly one hundred and seventy pages.

Already, you will have been made to realize something of the tremendous debt which we owe to the Apostle of the Gentiles: nowhere is this more evident than in his teaching on grace. One has only to recall the number of prayers and hymns in regular use in our worship which reflect such teaching.

The Greek word corresponding to our English word "grace" is *charis*. In origin, *charis* represents that which brings *chara*, "joy", and hence stands for "graciousness", "charm" or "attractiveness". An example of this use is to be found in Homer's *Odyssey*, where the goddess Athene made Odysseus "greater and more mighty to behold, and from his head caused deep curling thick locks to flow, like the hyacinth flower. And as when some skilful man overlays gold upon silver, even so did Athene shed grace about his head and shoulders. Then to the shore of the sea went Odysseus apart, and sat down, glowing in beauty and grace".[2]

From this basic meaning *charis* came to denote "goodwill", "kindly feeling" or "favour". Under the régime of an Eastern despot, such goodwill or favour on the part of the sovereign was essential if a subject wanted to keep his head on his shoulders. And not only under Eastern despots: for does not Scott in *Kenilworth* speak of "the marks of grace which Elizabeth from time to time showed the young Raleigh?"[3], and I need hardly

---
[1] J. Moffatt, *Grace in the New Testament*, p. 131.
[2] *The Odyssey of Homer* VI. 232-237 (translated by Butcher and Lang).
[3] W. Scott, *Kenilworth* XVII.

remind you that when under the English queen's successor such marks of grace came to an end, so too did Sir Walter!

We find in the Septuagint version of the Old Testament, in a book like Genesis, the phrase *heurein charin*, "to find favour", that is the favour which an inferior finds in the eyes of his superior, the Greek translators using *charis* to render the Hebrew *chēn*, a word connected with *chānan*), which means "to incline towards" and so "to favour".

As yet, you will see, we have had nothing to match the fullness and richness of *charis* in the New Testament, where it signifies not simply "favour" but *"unearned"* or *"undeserved* favour", and as such holds an important place in the Pauline vocabulary of justification.

St. Paul, who never ceased to forget that he owed his conversion to Christianity to divine grace, is among New Testament writers the *theologian of grace*. The Greek word *charis* is found no less than 101 times in his letters, whereas it occurs only about 50 times in the remainder of the New Testament, and never at all in the Gospels of St. Mark and St. Matthew. From this it is obvious that *charis*, "grace", is predominantly a Pauline word, and a leading idea essential to a right understanding of the good news. To quote Dr. J. K. Mozley: "Grace appears as that *regnant word of the Pauline theology* in which is contained the answer to the fact and problem of sin, bound up with the Incarnation and cross of the Son of God, and linked on with the extension of the Gospel to the Gentiles".[4]

The fundamental place of grace for St. Paul in the extension of the Gospel to the Gentiles is brought out in a lengthy and valuable note on the meaning of the word *charis* by Dr. J. Armitage Robinson in his commentary on the Epistle to the Ephesians, where he writes:

"There can be little doubt that the new and special use of *charis* in Paul's writings was closely connected with his missionary efforts, and that he did more than any one to develop the meaning of *charis* as a theological term. To him we owe the emphasis on the *freeness* of the divine favour, which is marked by the contrast of *charis* with *opheilema*, 'debt', and with *ergon* in the sense of meritorious 'work'; and the emphasis on the *universality* of the divine favour, which included Gentiles as well as Jews, in contrast to 'the law' which was the discipline of Israel." [5]

---

[4] *Essays Catholic and Critical*, p. 230.
[5] J. Armitage Robinson, *Ephesians*, p. 224.

We must now consider in more detail the various aspects of grace in St. Paul's letters:

(1) *The Grace of God*

If you study the superscriptions or introductions to the various Pauline letters in the New Testament, you will find that with only slight variations his form of greeting is as follows:

"Grace to you and peace from God the Father".

Grace then is "of God". Moreover, he speaks of grace as a gift bestowed by God on himself, as when he writes "I was made a minister according to the gift of God's grace which was given me" (*Eph.* 3: 7); and on others as well, as when in drawing the attention of the members of the church at Corinth to the generosity of the Macedonian Christians he attributes that generosity to "the grace of God" (*2 Cor.* 8: 1), and tells those same members that others long for and pray for them because of the surpassing grace of God in them (*2 Cor.* 9: 14).

(2) *The Grace of Christ*

Dr. C. L. Mitton in an admirable article on "Grace", to which I owe much, says: "God is the source from which grace comes to man. Jesus Christ is the God-ordained means by which this grace most effectively reaches man in his need."[6] Turn again to those superscriptions or introductions to the Pauline letters, and what do you find:

"Grace to you and peace from God the Father *and our Lord Jesus Christ*".

In *Rom.* 5: 15, St. Paul refers to the "grace of God and the free gift in the grace of . . . Jesus Christ"; while the words "The grace of our Lord Jesus Christ be with you", or something like them, are generally part of the closing farewell to his letters. It is however, *2 Cor.* 8: 9 which brings out most fully all that is meant by the grace of Christ—

"You know the grace of our Lord Jesus Christ, that though he was rich, yet for your sake"—and there are certain Greek manuscripts which have the reading "for *our* sake", since if anyone knew the personal experience of the grace of Christ it was St. Paul himself—"he became poor, so that by his poverty you might become rich".

The grace of Christ displayed itself in a gracious deed: that extra-

---

[6] C. L. Mitton, Article "Grace" in *Interpreter's Dictionary of the Bible*, Vol. II, p. 464.

ordinarily generous act of self-renunciation on his part, with all that it entailed, in order that he might bring salvation to a race utterly unworthy of it—"amazing grace" indeed!

(3) *Grace in relation to Man's Need*

Grace is given to man, says St. Paul, in order to enable him to achieve what he could not possibly do by himself. Here we must note how in St. Paul's teaching it is particularly associated with Justification: that is to say, God's acceptance of man as righteous and free from guilt.

This is the theme of the most theological of all St. Paul's letters, the *Epistle to the Romans*, where he describes in a vivid way in the first chapter the utter failure on the part of the Gentiles to make the grade. "Yes" would have been the reaction of the Jews of his day, "but *we* have the Law, and by fulfilling its commands a man may gain acceptance with God". "Not so", replies St. Paul in chapters 2 and 3, and concludes that "all men, both Jews and Greeks, are under the power of sin" (3: 9); "None is righteous, no, not one" (3: 10). It was into this apparently hopeless situation that God himself stepped and took action through Christ, with the result that although all of us have sinned, we are all "justified by God's grace as a gift, through the redemption which is in Christ Jesus" (3: 24). Justification is often said to be "by faith", though it is not strictly faith which justifies, but rather the grace of God which faith grasps.

Nowhere is the meaning of grace in relation to man's need so clearly brought out as in St. Paul's *Epistle to the Romans*. But his teaching on this important aspect of grace is not confined to that letter. In what may be one of the latest and most mature of his letters, the *Epistle to the Ephesians*, he attributes salvation to the action of God's grace: "By grace you have been saved" (*Eph.* 2: 5). A little later the same phrase is taken up again, but this time in association with faith: "By grace you have been saved, through faith" (2: 8).

If grace gives salvation to sinners, it also brings to Christians particular tasks in the service of God and their fellow-men. In St. Paul's own case, it was by the grace of God that he was called to his apostleship to the Gentiles, as well as equipped with the resources necessary for that task. Thus, the *Epistle to the Ephesians* refers to "the stewardship of God's grace that was given to me for you" (3: 2). Again, in *1 Corinthians* 15: 10, St. Paul writes: "By the grace of God I am what I am, and his grace toward me was not in vain"; and he then, in the same verse, proceeds to tell the

Corinthians that he had worked harder than any of the apostles, though he is careful to add "it was not I, but the grace of God with me".

There is, incidentally, a slight, though not unimportant variation of reading as regards the original Greek of this verse: not unimportant because it has a real bearing on St. Paul's doctrine of grace. According to the best Greek manuscripts of the New Testament, like that of the Codex Sinaiticus in the British Museum, the Greek reads *he charis tou Theou sun emoi*, which must be translated as I gave it, "the grace of God with me": that is to say, the divine grace and St. Paul himself were working together in mutual co-operation. On the other hand, some Greek manuscripts have the reading *hē charis tou Theou hē sun emoi*, a reading that is followed in some of our English translations like the Revised Standard Version, and which has to be rendered as "the grace of God which is with me". This reading, followed as we might expect by the sixteenth century Reformer, John Calvin, suggests that grace was the sole worker and that no credit whatever was due to St. Paul himself. But grace is not meant to take away our human responsibility, or to reduce us to the level of puppets. This surely cannot be emphasized too strongly.

While the ordinary Christian believer may not be called to apostleship there are other endowments which he can bring to the Church's corporate life: endowments which are described as *charismata*, that is *"grace-gifts"*, and which "differ according to the grace given to us" (*Rom.* 12: 6). The Second Vatican Council described them as "special graces", distributed among the faithful of every rank; and according to *Rom.* 12: 6 they include such gifts as prophecy, service and teaching. To these St. Paul adds in *1 Cor.* 12: 30, the gifts of healing and speaking with tongues. Regarding the latter, in these days when through the Charismatic or Pentecostal movement we are hearing a good deal about "speaking with tongues", it is salutary that we should have this reminder that whenever this occurs it is a *"grace-gift"*: and therefore gives no occasion for any sense of pride, superiority or exclusiveness.

(4) *Grace and its Contrasts*

Because man's acceptance with God is entirely God's doing—to quote once more our opening words: "All is of Grace and Grace is for all"—we must not be surprised to find that St. Paul draws sharp contrasts between grace and those things which are opposed to it. So:

(*a*) The Law is seen as the reverse of grace. Whereas for the Jew the ideal was to be "under the law", Paul declares in *Rom.* 6: 15 that for the Christian believer it is to be *"under grace".* The Greek word *hupo,* translated as "under", means "under the power" or "sovereignty" of something. "Law and Grace", says Dr. Moffatt, "are viewed as incompatible systems of religion. To toy with the former is to invalidate the latter, from which Christ came to free the soul." [7]

(*b*) Works, that is human achievements, are set in contrast to Grace: for, as St. Paul says in *Rom.* 11: 6: "If it is by grace, it is no longer on the basis of works; otherwise grace would no longer be grace". This is something which we in this country with its strong Pelagian outlook—Pelagius was a British monk of the fourth century, who taught that if a man tried hard enough he could be saved by his own efforts without the aid of God's grace—find it difficult to understand: witness the popularity long enjoyed by Rudyard Kipling's poem "If".

(*c*) Sin is contrasted with grace. "Are we", says St. Paul in *Rom.* 6: 1, "to continue in sin that grace may abound? By no means!" It is sin, or disobedience to the divine will, which makes us unacceptable to God; whereas grace makes us accepted in spite of our sin.

(5) *Characteristics of Grace*

It remains for us to consider certain characteristics of grace to which St. Paul draws attention:

(*a*) It is described by him as "abounding" or "overflowing"—or as Charles Wesley later put it in one of his best-loved hymns, "Plenteous grace": "grace to cover all my sin". "Law", writes St. Paul in *Rom.* 5: 20, "came in to increase the trespass: but where sin increased, grace abounded all the more". It was this characteristic of grace which provided the seventeenth century John Bunyan with the title of one of the more familiar of his works, *Grace Abounding to the Chief of Sinners.*

(*b*) It is a *free gift*, never man's due or reward. In *Eph.* 2: 8, it is called "the gift of God". The Greek word used here is *dōron,* which means "gift"; but more often we find the stronger word *dōrea,* meaning *"free* gift". The latter is a word which carries the idea of "gratis", "without price", "in the manner of a gift"—all emphasizing the *gift*-character of grace. While our English translations make the difference clear in *Rom.* 5: 15, where *dōrea* is rendered as "the *free* gift", it is a pity that in other places like

[7] *Op. cit.,* p. 182.

2 *Cor.* 9: 15 and *Eph.* 3: 7, 4: 7 it is simply translated as "gift". Paul then constantly emphasises the *given-ness* of grace.

(c) It is through faith. Grace, as we have seen, is frequently associated with faith by which a person responds to the offer of God's grace. Here, of course, we meet with the old question: "Which came first: Faith or grace?" Indeed, theologians differ as to how far faith itself is the gift of God's grace, as St. Paul himself seems to suggest in *Phil.* 1: 29, where he writes: "It has been granted to you that for the sake of Christ you should . . . believe in him". To quote Dr. C. L. Mitton once again:

"Something of a paradox marks Christian experience at this point. The believer is utterly sure that 'it is all God's doing', but he also knows that at some point he has had to say 'yes' when he might have said 'no'." [8]

(d) It is spontaneous. The spontaneity of the gift of grace becomes clear when we realize that there is no waiting until we have reached a certain standard before we can receive it. "God shows his love for us in that while we were yet sinners Christ died for us", says St. Paul in *Rom.* 5: 8.

(e) It has a great appeal. There is no need to dwell at length on the immense appeal of this free and spontaneous gift of divine grace for St. Paul himself and for men and women of successive generations. Nowhere is this more clearly brought out than by some of our eighteenth century English hymn-writers: for example, Philip Doddridge who, as he meditated on *Eph.* 2: 5, was moved to set down the lines:

"Grace! 'tis a charming sound,
Harmonious to the ear";

or the Evangelical John Newton, expounding on what he called

"Amazing grace! (how sweet the sound)"

wrote:

"How precious did that grace appear
The hour I first believ'd."

(f) It may, nevertheless, be resisted. Those who hold the doctrine of irresistible grace and the Calvinistic teaching on predestination turn for support to *Rom.* 9–11 where St. Paul appears to suggest that God determines the destiny of individuals before birth, and even speaks in *Rom.* 11: 5 of "a remnant chosen by grace". Many like the Gnostics of the second century with their

[8] *Op. cit.,* p. 466.

exclusive religious claims, have found the doctrine of election congenial.

We must not, however, take these chapters out of their context, nor overlook the fact that while St. Paul, in company with Old Testament prophets like Jeremiah, lays down the principle that God may choose and reject whomever he wishes, yet he is very careful to point out that actually that is not his method. Rejection comes not through God, but through the refusal of man to respond to the divine grace. Despite the wonder expressed by some pious writers that anyone should reject God's grace, we know in fact that all too many do: as St. Paul himself allows when he says in *Gal.* 2: 21 that it is possible to "nullify" or "set at nought" the grace of God; and again when, in 5: 4 of the same letter, he admonishes the Christians of Galatia because they have "fallen away" from grace.

* * *

It may come as something of a surprise to those of us who have been brought up to regard the Sacraments of the Church as the special "means of grace" to discover that neither St. Paul nor any other New Testament writer actually associates *charis* with the sacraments. It is, however, not difficult to understand how there must naturally have grown this connexion between grace and the sacraments as the particular means by which Christians are enabled to live the spiritual life; and also the distinction made between "actual grace"—the power given to us in moments of special need, and "habitual grace"—the power given us for sanctification through those means of grace the Sacraments.

In later Christian history there were two periods when St. Paul's teaching on grace was of particular concern: first during the time of St. Augustine of Hippo, and secondly in the sixteenth century Reformation.

St. Augustine, who is remembered as pre-eminently the theologian of grace, was led to formulate his doctrine in the face of an attempt to water down the teaching of the New Testament and to substitute man's own unaided efforts for the grace of God: the Pelagian heresy to which I have already referred. Because St. Augustine, like St. Paul before him, knew from personal experience what grace meant, he could not compromise in so serious a matter as this. But while St. Augustine repeated what St. Paul had said about grace, he went too far, and in his remarks on irresistible grace and predestination unfortunately prepared the way for the extreme opinions held by Calvin and his disciples, not least when it came to the matter of total depravity.

In the teachings of the medieval Schoolmen, further distinctions were made between "prevenient grace"—the grace preceding an act and enabling one to want to do it; "concomitant grace"—the grace which works with one and enables one actually to perform the act; and "subsequent grace"—as the name suggests, the grace which follows from doing it. These theologians also talked about "infused grace", and claimed that divine grace had to be mediated through the sacraments administered by a priesthood which was in communion with Rome.

In the face of such developments, it seemed to the Reformers of the sixteenth century that it was their task to get back to the Pauline teaching on justification "by faith"—though, as I pointed out earlier, it is not strictly faith which justifies, but rather the grace of God which faith grasps. In one of his early theological works Luther, in dealing with *Rom.* 3 and the contrast which St. Paul drew there between grace and the Law, writes:

"Here I quite properly understand grace as the favourable dispensation of God towards us, as ought to be the case, and not as a quality of the soul as our modernists"—he was referring to St. Thomas Aquinas!—"have taught." "This grace effects a true peace of mind eventually so that a man is healed of his disease and knows in addition that he has a gracious God. This is what puts marrow into the bones!" [9]

Good as the intention of Luther and other sixteenth century Reformers may have been, the question raised today in the light of the Ecumenical Movement and the discussions between representatives of the various Churches on such matters as the nature of the Church and the function of the ministry, is whether those Reformers—and perhaps particularly Calvin—were right in their interpretation of Paul's teaching on grace?

Before I end, there is one other characteristic of grace in St. Paul's teaching to which I would draw your attention: and that is its *power-like* quality. For how else are we to understand the words of *2 Cor.* 12: 9: "My grace is sufficient for you: for my power is made perfect in weakness"? As I recall the strength which I gained from those words on the eve of my ordination to the priesthood, and the help which they have been in the years between that day and this, there is no verse rather than that on which I would end my exposition of St. Paul's teaching on grace.

"O God, who declarest thy almighty power most chiefly in

---

[9] M. Luther, *Answer to Latomus in Early Theological Works*, Library of Christian Classics, Vol. XVI, p. 348.

shewing mercy and pity; Mercifully grant unto us such a measure of thy grace, that we, running the way of thy commandments, may obtain thy gracious promises, and be made partakers of thy heavenly treasure; through Jesus Christ our Lord. Amen." [10]

[10] Collect for Trinity XI.

CHAPTER VIII

ST. PAUL'S TEACHING ON BAPTISM AND THE SPIRIT

by
Geoffrey Lampe

IF we want to understand St. Paul's view of the relationship between the Christian experience of the Holy Spirit and the sacrament of baptism we must try to see it within the wider framework of his very profound and highly original reinterpretation of the ancient concept of the Spirit of God or "Holy Spirit".

"Spirit" is one of many terms which were used in the Old Testament to express the idea of God's "outreach" towards the world of his creation. They can be called "bridge" terms, for they point to the activity of transcendent Deity "impinging upon" creaturely beings, and especially to that approach, address or self-communication of the Creator which is experienced by human beings as personal encounter with God. They include the concrete physical images of the "hand" or "arm" or "finger" of God (note that in *Luke* 11: 20 and the parallel passage *Matthew* 12: 28 God's "finger" and God's "Spirit" are synonymous). These metaphors attempt to put into words an experience of being touched; God seems to reach out and touch, move, guide, protect, heal, bless, or. with his arm outstretched, to intervene in the affairs of nations, executing justice and vindicating the oppressed. At a rather deeper level of personal experience, the "Word" of God addresses men, especially through prophets to whom this Word has come; and God's Word is the communication and expression of his creative "Wisdom". Another "bridge" concept is that of "angel": not, in the earlier books of the Old Testament, a created intermediary but, like God's "hand", "Word" and "Wisdom", his own personal self-communication, God himself as disclosed to, and experienced by, man. "Spirit" is a metaphor of physical breath. It suggests the communication of life, and it is thus a term which expresses a particularly intimate relationship between God and man, for "Spirit" does not merely address us in an external fashion from beyond ourslves but enters, possesses, indwells, and may become the principle of new and higher dimensions of life.

"Spirit" means God inspiring, whether it be the skilful artist (*Exod.* 35: 31), the warrior (*Jdg.* 6: 34), Samson in his feats of strength (*Jdg.* 14: 6), the prophet-preacher (*Mic.* 3: 8), or the king, especially the ideal ruler, the Branch of Jesse foreseen by Isaiah (11: 2). God's Spirit is God's own indwelling, and so for the Psalmist it is one and the same thing to pray "Cast me not away from thy presence" and "take not thy Holy Spirit from me" (*Ps.* 51: 11).

For St. Paul, too, the Spirit is God's active presence, bringing inspiration, power and special endowments; but now this presence can be defined in a new way, for the Holy Spirit in Christian experience is God making the risen Christ present to the individual believer and to the believing Church. The activity of the Spirit is the mode in which Christ is made contemporary with, and present to, his people now that his corporeal presence has been withdrawn: through the medium of the Spirit Christ dwells in the faithful so as to become the principle of that new quality of life which is Christ-like life, life in Christ, life motivated and empowered by the indwelling Spirit, the foretaste and first instalment of the resurrection life which is the object of Christian hope.

St. Paul's letters to the Thessalonians, probably his earliest, contain comparatively few allusions to the Holy Spirit, but these point the way to the more developed thought of the letters to Corinth, Galatia and Rome. The Holy Spirit is the dynamic power of God which gives the Christian mission its driving force and converts men through the proclamation of the gospel (*1 Thess.* 1: 5). A characteristic sign of the working of the Spirit is joy: St. Paul's converts at Thessalonica "followed the example set by us and by the Lord; the welcome you gave the message meant grave suffering for you, yet you rejoiced in the Holy Spirit". This recalls the description of the Kingdom of God which he gives to the Romans (14: 17): it is "justice, peace, and joy inspired by the Holy Spirit", and the famous passage in *Galatians* (5: 22) where he says that "the harvest of the Spirit is love, joy, peace, patience, kindness, goodness, fidelity, gentleness, and self-control". In other words, the Spirit reproduces in believers the distinctively Christ-like virtues. In this enumeration of the characteristics of the Christ-like character love precedes joy, and in *1 Thess.* 4: 6-9 the inspiration of the Spirit is directly related to love of the brethren; to reject one's brother and violate his rights is to reject God who gives us his Holy Spirit. This passage prepares the way for the teaching of *1 Cor.* 13, that the supreme manifestation of the Spirit, the essential gift or "operation" without which there can be no authentically

Christian life, is "charity", that is, spontaneous, unselfish love which reproduces at the human level the divine love disclosed in Christ.

These are largely new, Christian, insights; but St. Paul still echoes the traditional assertion that the inspiration of the Spirit is specially exhibited in the gift of prophecy. "Do not quench the Spirit (N.E.B.: "Do not stifle inspiration"), and do not despise prophetic utterances" (*1 Thess.* 5: 19). Prophecy is parallel to "word of mouth" and "written letter" as a source of apostolic teaching (*2 Thess.* 2: 2), and in writing to the Corinthians St. Paul makes it very clear that prophecy is a higher gift, or operation, of the Spirit than "tongues". This is because prophecy is immediately intelligible and therefore serves to build up, or edify, the Christian community, whereas "tongues" are a gift of the Spirit for private and individual personal devotion (*1 Cor.* 14: 2–6). We know little about the nature of Christian prophecy, but the association of prophets with apostles and teachers as Christian missionaries indicates that the prophetic inspiration was directly related to the preaching of Christ; it seems probable that the discernment of the Christological reference of Old Testament prophecies and their fulfilment in Christ and in the Church was an important part of the ministry of the prophets. One point is of special significance; St. Paul believes that even the utterances of apparently inspired prophets are subject to testing. They must not be accepted as infallible, for it is not the manner in which a prophet speaks, whether in ecstasy or in any other abnormal condition, but the content of his utterance which determines whether he is truly inspired or not. There were apparently some prophets who cried "A curse on Jesus!" (*1 Cor.* 12: 3). Who these were is obscure; possibly they were Jewish prophets and teachers trying to mount a counter-attack to the Christian mission in the synagogues of the Dispersion. St. Paul points out that no one who says this can be genuinely inspired by the Spirit of God. On the other hand, no one can affirm the primitive Christian creed, "Jesus is Lord", unless he is under the Spirit's influence. The sense of being inspired, and the outward appearance of being inspired, do not, therefore, exempt anyone from being "brought to the test" (*1 Thess.* 5: 20–21).

The Thessalonian epistles also introduce the fact that the Spirit sanctifies, or, as the New English Bible translates it, "consecrates" the believer, that is to say, the Spirit makes us God's own possession, members of his people who are dedicated to his service (*2 Thess.* 2: 13). This thought is developed with direct reference to baptism in *1 Cor.* 6: 11: in our baptism we are "justified" or brought into a right relationship with God, and "sanctified" or made one of his holy (i.e., consecrated) people (justification and sanctification being virtually identical here), in the name of the Lord Jesus and the Spirit of our God.

On a more profound level St. Paul speaks of the Spirit as the source of true wisdom (*1 Cor.* 2: 10–16). The Spirit is no less than God's own inner self-consciousness, communicated to men and enabling them to understand the purpose of God for their salvation. Isaiah had asked, "Who knows the mind of the Lord?"; Paul returns the astonishing answer, "We possess the mind of Christ", because the Holy Spirit reproduces and re-presents in Christian people, in so far as they are open to his influence, the Christ-like mind and character. St. Paul does not often refer to the tradition of the actual teaching of Jesus; he believes that it is not so much by referring back to the remembered sayings of the Lord as by following the guidance of the Spirit in the Christian community that we can discern the mind of Christ. Indeed, the Spirit and the "mind of Christ" are practically synonymous. The individual believer can possess this gift; Paul claims himself to "have the Spirit of God" and to be able to judge with the mind of Christ (*1 Cor.* 7: 40). But it is primarily the Church collectively which is, as it were, the temple in which the Spirit is enshrined (*1 Cor.* 3: 16). Within this community the individuals have their own special *charismata*, gifts, or modes, of the operation of the one Spirit. These vary according to the individual's natural talents and potentialities. They may take the form of prophecy, or teaching, or miracle-working, or healing, or gifts of administration and leadership, or the gift of tongues. All should serve to witness to Christ and build up the community in his service; and it is significant that, judged by their usefulness for this purpose, "tongues" come at the bottom of the Pauline list (*1 Cor.* 12: 28–31). The greatest of all the workings of the Spirit is love. Without this all other gifts are useless (*1 Cor.* 13). Hence "fellowship in the Holy Spirit" is indissolubly linked with the "grace of the Lord Jesus Christ" and the "love of God" (*2 Cor.* 13: 14).

In all these aspects the indwelling Spirit is the pledge of that new life in Christ for which we hope when our redemption has been completed and we have been refashioned according to the pattern of Christ. Our present experience of the Spirit on this side of the grave is the "earnest" of our future hope: the first instalment which guarantees the full payment, the firstfruits that are the sure token of the final harvest (*2 Cor.* 1: 22, *Rom.* 8: 23). To receive the indwelling of God's Spirit now is to be assured of the promise of the eschatological fulfilment, for the Spirit is God's seal, the sign that we belong to him, which he has placed upon us to mark us as his people (*Eph.* 4: 30). This is so because for practical purposes it is one and the same thing to say that the Spirit dwells in us and that Christ dwells in us. We need not suppose that Paul intends to suggest that there is an absolute, ontological, identification of the Spirit with Christ. When he tells his readers (*2 Cor.* 3: 17) that "the Lord is the Spirit", he is working out an elaborate typological exegesis of *Exodus* 3: 29-35. When Moses descended from Sinai with the tables of the Law, his face shone, and he put a veil over his face so that the Israelites might approach him and talk with him without being dazzled and overawed by the divine splendour; but when Moses turned to the Lord to speak with him within the tabernacle he removed the veil from his face. St. Paul is working out an elaborate comparison between the old covenant of the Law and the new covenant of the gospel, and between Moses as the minister of the old covenant and the apostolic ministers of the gospel. The Jews who have rejected the gospel cannot see the glory of God; when they read the Law of Moses a veil is still spread over their minds, but if they should turn to the Lord (as Moses did in the tabernacle) then the veil will be removed. Now, says St. Paul, to turn to the Lord means, in their case, to turn from the dispensation of Law to the new dispensation of the Spirit; in his interpretation of Exodus "the Lord" means "the Spirit". So the New English Bible gives the sense very clearly when it translates St. Paul's words: "Now the Lord of whom this passage speaks is the Spirit". Nevertheless, although he does not say that the word "Spirit" actually means exactly the same thing as the word "Christ", St. Paul is quite clear that for practical purposes they are identical. To be "in Christ" is to be indwelt, or possessed, by the Spirit.

Since the primary work of the Spirit is to re-present and reproduce Christ in the community of the Church, so as to make it Christ's body, and in the individual believer, so as to "shape him to the likeness of God's Son" (cf. *Rom.* 8: 29), the great gift that the Spirit brings us is the assurance that we are children of God. "To prove that you are sons, God has sent into our hearts the Spirit of his Son, crying 'Abba! Father!' " (*Gal.* 4: 6). This means that God's Spirit, sent into our hearts, prays within us and through us the characteristic prayer of Jesus, who addressed God, uniquely, with the familiar, and almost homely, word with which, in all probability, the Lord's Prayer opened in the Aramaic language which Jesus spoke: "Abba". So, writes St. Paul in one of his greatest passages about the Spirit, "You are not in the flesh but in the Spirit, if only God's Spirit dwells in you; and if a man does not possess Christ's Spirit he does not belong to Christ. But if Christ dwells in you, then although the body is dead because of sin, yet the Spirit is life because you have been justified.... For all who are moved by the Spirit of God are sons of God. The Spirit you have received is not a spirit of slavery leading you back into a life of fear, but a Spirit that makes us sons, enabling us to cry 'Abba! Father!'. In that cry the Spirit of God joins with our spirit in testifying that we are God's children" (*Rom.* 8: 9–10, 14–16).

To be in Christ is to be indwelt by the Spirit; and St. Paul is clear that the sacrament by which we come to be in Christ, that is, to be made members of the Christian society, the body of Christ and the temple of the Spirit, is baptism. He does not refer to it very often, but it would be the greatest mistake to infer from *1 Cor.* 1: 13–17 that he depreciated its importance. In that passage he is complaining of the tendency of the Corinthian Christians to form party factions, splitting the unity of the local church. To say, "I belong to Paul", "I am for Apollos", "I am for Cephas", is in fact an absurdity, for "was it Paul who was crucified for you? Was it in the name of Paul that you were baptized?" So anxious is he to remind them that they were not baptized in the name of any human missionary, so as to become that person's devoted follower, but simply, and all alike, into Christ's name, that he thanks God he scarcely baptized any of them. The task of St. Paul himself, as a pioneer missionary, was to preach the gospel; the administration of baptism was apparently entrusted to others. This did not mean that baptism was of secondary importance; the whole point of his argument is that every convert who responded to the apostle's preaching was baptized, and that this baptism made the convert Christ's man, bound to Christ in loyalty and service. And to come to belong to Christ is to receive the Spirit to dwell in one's heart as the pledge of the future hope of total redemption (*2 Cor.* 1: 22).

"Through faith", St. Paul reminds the Galatians, "you are all sons of God in Christ Jesus. Baptized into union with him, you have all put on Christ as a garment", and in this union with Christ all earthly distinctions such as race and social status are transcended (*Gal.* 3: 26–28). Baptism sacramentally effects a transition into the life of sonship to God in Christ, which is life in the Spirit.

It does this because it is an effective sign, and dramatic representation, of Christ's death, burial and resurrection. It therefore signifies the Christian believer's death to his self-orientated, God-rejecting life, and his entry into a new life of sonship to God in which the Spirit produces the "harvest" of love, joy, peace, and the other Christ-like qualities. In Old Testament symbolism water had a double significance. In one aspect it stood for death and destruction; the imagery of the Flood, the "deep", the watery chaos of *Genesis* 1: 2, the sea which, through the mythical agency of a great fish or sea monster, swallowed Jonah, portrays the grave and the underworld where the shades of the dead go down into silence. In the other, opposite, sense water stands for life, and the imagery speaks of life and hope and newness springing up in what was the deadness of a waterless desert. To the Christian apostle this double symbolism of water signified the death and resurrection of Christ which the believer figuratively shares when he sacramentally goes down into the grave and rises to new life in Christ through the water of baptism. "When we were baptized into union with Christ Jesus we were baptized into his death. By baptism we were buried with him, and lay dead, in order that, as Christ was raised from the dead in the splendour of the Father, so also we might set our feet upon the new path of life" (*Rom.* 6: 3-4). As we have already seen, this new way of life is opened to us by the guidance of the Spirit.

More central in the Pauline understanding of baptism than in the thought of the other New Testament writers is this interpretation of baptism as a sacramental sign of our union with Christ in death and resurrection. "In baptism", the Colossians are told, "you were buried with him, in baptism also you were raised to life with him through your faith in the active power of God who raised him from the dead". And, because baptism signifies that dying to sin and rising to the life of the Spirit which the Christian has to re-enact day by day, it is a rebirth, a "regeneration" in the sense of a new beginning of life in the community of Christ's body. So the probably post-Pauline epistle to Titus speaks of baptism as an act of God who "saved us through the water of rebirth and the renewing power of the Holy Spirit" (*Tit.* 3: 5).

In view of our own controversies we should dearly like to know whether infant baptism was practised in the Pauline churches and whether he approved of it; but St. Paul says nothing about this subject directly, and it would be an illegitimate inference from the fact that he baptized the "household of Stephanas" (*1 Cor.* 1: 16) to suppose that infants, or even children, were included in it. All we can safely say, since in a pioneer missionary situation such as the Pauline letters envisage baptism would inevitably be normally of adult believers, is that for St. Paul baptism admits to the Church, and the Church is the society in which and to which Christ is present through, or in the mode of, the Holy Spirit. We must form our own conclusions as to whether, and if so in what circumstances, infants may be admitted into that society. St. Paul certainly offers us no ground for the view that for infants, or for anyone else, there can be any kind of substitute for baptism; he knows nothing of infant blessing or dedication.

CHAPTER IX

ST. PAUL'S TEACHING ON THE HOLY EUCHARIST

by
Eric Mascall

IN considering this subject some preliminary points need to be made:

(1) There is no reason to suppose that St. Paul's eucharistic teaching was substantially different from that of the early Church as a whole. In *1 Cor.* 11: 23 he says that he had delivered to the church in Corinth that which he had received from the Lord, and the close parallel between his account of the institution of the Eucharist and the accounts in the synoptic gospels (Matthew, Mark and Luke) makes it plain that this was no private revelation but the tradition which he had received from the Lord through the Church, which, as he emphasizes elsewhere, is the Lord's Body.

(2) St. Paul's explicit teaching about the Eucharist is confined to two chapters (10 and 11) of *1 Corinthians,* where he is dealing with certain disorders which had crept into the eucharistic practice of the Corinthian church. Had these disorders not occurred, we should have no explicit evidence that St. Paul had ever heard of the Eucharist. This shows how very dangerous it is to assume, as so many have assumed, that anything which is not definitely mentioned in the New Testament either did not exist or was of no importance in the primitive church. Writing materials were expensive and there was no need to tell people what they already knew, unless some special reason arose for this. Thus some of the most important and universally accepted aspects of the Church's life may be virtually unmentioned in the Scriptures. This is one of the reasons why we need to have respect to history and tradition if our use of the Bible is to be fruitful. We ought perhaps to be grateful to the disorderly Corinthian Christians for having evoked St. Paul's reminders of the teaching which both he and they had "received"!

(3) When this has been recognized, we can then see how, in spite of there being so little explicit mention of the Eucharist in the New Testament, the language of the Epistles and Gospels, *Acts*

and *Revelation* are full of eucharistic overtones. Dom Gregory Dix, on p. 4 of his great work *The Shape of the Liturgy,* has listed many of these: "By the time the New Testament came to be written", he tells us, "the Eucharist already illuminated everything concerning Jesus for his disciples—his Person, his Messianic office, his miracles, his death and the redemption that he brought."

Turning now to chapters 10 and 11 of St. Paul's first letter to the church at Corinth, we are impressed by two main themes. The first is that of the intimate connexion between the eucharistic meal and the very existence of the Church as the redeemed community; there is no suggestion whatever that a man can be a Christian on his own, apart from his membership of the Church. The second theme is that of the sacred character of the eucharistic elements. And these two themes are interwoven. "The cup of blessing which we bless, is it not a participation in the blood of Christ? The bread which we break, is it not a participation in the body of Christ?" (10: 16). And immediately the apostle makes the link between the eucharistic body and the ecclesial body: "Because there is one loaf, we who are many are one body, for we all partake of the same loaf" (10: 17). And it is for this reason that it is disgraceful for Christians to take part in meals held in pagan temples or knowingly to eat food which has been offered in pagan sacrifices; not that the food in itself has been changed by the pagan rites. Neither the food offered to idols nor the idol itself is "anything" (10: 19). But, says St. Paul, "what pagans sacrifice they offer to demons and not to God", and "I do not want you to be partners with demons. You cannot drink the cup of the Lord and the cup of demons, You cannot partake of the table of the Lord and the table of demons" (10: 20, 21). However, if the food in the pagan rites has not been changed, the food in the Christian rite certainly has been: "Whoever eats the bread or drinks the cup of the Lord in an unworthy manner will be guilty of profaning the body and blood of the Lord. . . . Anyone who eats and drinks without discerning the body eats and drinks judgment upon himself" (11: 27, 29).

Like the synoptics, St. Paul does not give a full account of the ritual which our Lord would have followed at the Last Supper, but contents himself with quoting the unexpected, and, to a Jew, shocking, words which he added to the rite, and by which he transformed it from a ceremonial Jewish blessing of food and drink to a sacrificial rite of universal significance identified with his death by crucifixion on the following day. Whether the Last Supper was literally a Passover meal is a matter of dispute (cf.

Dix, pp. 50ff.), though it certainly took place at the time and in the setting of the Passover, the great annual commemoration of the deliverance of the Jewish people from Egypt centuries before; no mention is made in any of the accounts of the passover lamb. What Christ did at the Last Supper was to bless the bread at the beginning of the meal in the customary way and then to declare, as he distributed it, that it was his body. Then at the end of the meal, when he had blessed the ceremonial cup with a prayer in which he would have given thanks to God for all his great work in creation and redemption, he gave it to his companions with the declaration that it was his blood of the new covenant (*or* the new covenant in his blood), poured out for many for the forgiveness of sins (*1 Cor.* 11: 23–25; *Matt.* 26: 26–28; *Mark* 14: 22–24; *Luke* 22: 17–19). (The precise wording varies in the different accounts, which have no doubt come down through the liturgical traditions of different Christian churches.) The two actions, of the bread and the cup, are tied together in St. Paul's account by the repeated command "Do this for my re-calling (*anamnesis*)". The word *anamnesis* has more than a merely psychological reference; it means a real making-present of an event which is chronologically past. Like the English word "re-calling", it has a double sense; in a court of law a witness may be asked to "recall" (i.e. to remember) an event which happened some time before, but also the witness may himself be "recalled" (i.e. be physically brought back and put in the witness-box again). It has sometimes been argued that the Greek word *poieite,* translated "do" in the phrase "do this", really means "offer" and has therefore a sacrificial meaning, but this is uncertain. The undoubtedly sacrificial words are "my blood of the covenant", which take us right back to *Exodus* 24. In that account Moses, after offering a sacrifice of oxen to ratify the covenant which God had made with Israel, threw the blood over the people with the words "Behold the blood of the covenant which the Lord has made with you in accordance with all these words" (*Exod.* 24: 3–8). So Jesus at the Last Supper was announcing that a new covenant (the new covenant which Jeremiah had foretold would be made in the hearts of his people (*Jer.* 31: 31ff.)) was now being made, not in the blood of dumb animals but in his own life-blood, and that this blood was not merely to be thrown over them in a purely external and symbolic application but was to be drunk by them and enter into their very substance. Furthermore, in Jewish thought the blood of a living animal was virtually identified with its life and the very idea of consuming blood was shocking to the Jews. Thus our Lord's command to drink his blood is an invitation to share in his very life. In his letter to the Corinthian church St. Paul does not go out of his way to expatiate on this Jewish background of the Eucharist. This may be one of the things that are not mentioned because they were familiar and undisputed. On the other hand, it is possible that he thought it was not of very much importance to Gentile Christians and would not mean very much to them. In any case, he restricts himself to reminding them of the two all-important sayings of the Lord, in connexion with the bread and the cup respectively, that these were his body and his blood, and that they were to "do this" as his re-calling. For, he wrote, with his mind on the Lord's return in glory at the last day, "as often as you eat this bread and drink the cup you proclaim the Lord's death until he comes" (*1 Cor.* 11: 26).

"About the other things", he concludes, "I will give directions when I come" (11: 34). We know that very early in the Church's history everything in the meal except the bread and the cup were withdrawn and made into a separate ceremony—the *agape* or "love"—so that the bread and the cup were left in immediate proximity and became the Eucharist as the Church has known it throughout her subsequent history. But the name "Eucharist"—"thanksgiving"—has remained to remind us that the central rite by which the Church has lived throughout the centuries took its rise in the occasion when a young Jewish rabbi, eating with his closest friends on the evening before his execution on a trumped-up charge of sedition, followed the prescribed Jewish custom of blessing food and drink by blessing God his Father for them and for all his works of creation and redemption, and added to it the totally unprescribed and unexpected declaration that the bread was his body and the wine was his blood.

This is virtually all that St. Paul says about the Eucharist in those of his writings that have come down to us, and we owe this to the *felix culpa* of the disorders at Corinth. And, as was said at the start, we have no reason to suppose that his eucharistic beliefs were different in any important respect from those of the primitive Church in general. So perhaps a better title than "St. Paul's Teaching on the Holy Eucharist" would be "The Eucharistic Teaching of the Primitive Church as expressed in the writings of St. Paul".

CHAPTER X

ST. PAUL'S TEACHING ON THE UNITY OF THE CHURCH

by

H. J. Carpenter

THE ecumenical movement and its work for Christian unity is not much more than fifty years old; we can therefore easily suppose that "unity" is a new and modern concern among Christian people. This is in fact true if we compare this movement with the outlook of the eighteenth and nineteenth centuries in which the existence of denominations opposed to, and/or ignorant of one another was accepted as a normal and natural situation by most Christian people. But if we go back further in history and indeed to New Testament times we find that the unity of the Christian community has been regarded as one of its basic and necessary features. I hope to show that, for St. Paul's thought and work as an apostle, unity in its different aspects was a built-in concern, arising out of the one basic Gospel which he preached.

When Paul was martyred in Rome about AD 65 the Christian Church consisted of a number of small scattered communities mostly along the eastern coastlands of the Mediterranean, with some in Greece and a few in the city of Rome and its neighbourhood. On the map the Church at this time would appear as a long thin line of separated dots coinciding with certain towns and cities. The people who made up these small local groups were all very recent converts; the Christian faith and way of life were new and strange, and also hard to maintain in a pagan environment. There were many difficulties in keeping these widely separated groups united internally and with one another. At Corinth, for example, there were "parties"; "I am Paul's man", "I am for Apollos", "I follow Peter" (*1 Cor.* 1: 12). Another threat was from Jewish converts or missionaries who said that Gentile converts must accept certain Jewish practices (chiefly circumcision) before they could become Christians. (See *Galatians*.) Further, all around them the contemporary world was full of religious ideas and movements, and it was easy for some of these to infiltrate a Christian congregation and distort the faith and life of its members, as well as introducing conflicts and divisions. This is the kind of situation revealed in the *Epistle to the Colossians*.

The letters of St. Paul show him fully aware of these dangers and determined to combat them energetically. At the cost of great physical effort and suffering (*2 Cor.* 11: 23–33), he was constantly travelling to visit these local communities, and apart from his personal visits he was always in communication with them through his own letters, through his assistants Timothy, Titus, and others, and also through the messengers or delegations sent to him by the local churches. His converts looked to him for pastoral care, for instruction in Christian faith and conduct, and for the settling of points in their community life where there was doubt or difficulty. St. Paul clearly regarded it as an essential part of his calling as an apostle to serve them in all these ways. His apostleship was, in fact, a focal point of unity for these young Christian congregations. Moreover, Paul insisted that they must feel real and practical concern for their brethren in other places. He and his assistants put a great deal of effort into raising a fund from some of the Greek congregations and others to help the "poor saints" in far-off Jerusalem. For him the obligation to give this form of "Christian Aid" arose directly out of the unity of the Jerusalem Church with the other local churches hundreds of miles away (*Rom.* 15: 25, *1 Cor.* 16: 1–4, *2 Cor.* 8 and 9). His vision is of a Church potentially universal, whose local congregations realize and give effect to their unity as a community of believing persons with mutual sharing and caring, and under apostolic guidance.

Why did unity matter and why did the apostle work so hard to maintain it and make it a reality? He would have said that this unity was required by the one gospel which he preached to them, the gospel of one crucified and risen Lord Jesus Christ. We must look a little more closely at what he said about this.

First we notice that this gospel as summarized in *1 Cor.* 15: 3ff. contains a reference to "the Scriptures". "Christ died for our sins according to the Scriptures." The reference is to what we call the books of the Old Testament. The coming and work of Christ were the climax and fulfilment of the revelation of himself which God had given to his ancient people, the church of Israel. When you became a Christian, if you had been a Jew, you already believed in "the Scriptures", and in God's revelation of himself to Israel as the one true and living God, the creator, alone to be worshipped, and active in history. If you were a Gentile convert, you had to "turn from idols to worship a living and true God" (*1 Thess.* 1: 9), as part of your turning to Jesus Christ, who was sent by God. To all Christians, whether Jews or Gentiles in origin, "the Scriptures" spoke of the God and Father of our Lord Jesus Christ, and contained the promise of the gospel to come. St. Paul assumes that Old Testament figures like Abraham, Isaac and Moses are known to the readers of his letters. Writing to the Christians in Corinth he, for example, can refer to the Israelites in the wilderness as "our ancestors" (*1 Cor.* 10: 1). The Gentiles (Greeks) in the congregation had to get used to the rather new idea of the ancient Israelites as their ancestors.

The gospel, then, came to these Pauline Christians with Scriptures, sacred books, which were read and spoken about in Christian worship, as they had been for two or more centuries previously in the Jewish synagogues, but now with the conviction that the ancient promises of God had been fulfilled in Christ. The Church started its life with the Old Testament Scriptures as its charter, and this volume was a bond of unity between the dispersed congregations, as it continued to be in the subsequent history of the Church. It witnessed to the ancient acts of God, of which the gospel was to be the fulfilment.

The gospel itself was centred in Jesus Christ who gave himself to be crucified for us, and rose again to be the living and glorified Lord of his people (e.g., *1 Cor.* 15: 4ff., *Rom.* 10: 9). Through him God had brought man into a new relation of reconciliation with himself and had thus revealed in a definite form his love and goodness. Through Christ men were offered a new life of sonship and grace which could be described as a new creation.

If in brief this was the "good news" and you wanted to accept it, what did St. Paul expect you to do? I think there is no doubt about the answer. You openly professed your faith in Christ crucified and risen, you were baptized, and entered into the Christian community. These three things were inseparable. Throughout his letters St. Paul assumes that all who believe have been baptized, and are members of their local Christian community. In all his messages he is concerned with the common life and appeals to the fact of the common faith and the common baptism. Membership of the Church is not for him an optional extra or a helpful support to the individual; it is the necessary expression of life in Christ, and the oneness of Christ's people arises from the one Lord, Jesus Christ, and the one Holy Spirit in which all Christians participate (*1 Cor.* 12: 11–13). The gospel itself meant a shared common life in which God's promises in Christ were accepted and began to be fulfilled. The basis of the common life was faith and baptism, which brought the members into unity in Christ and in common participation in the Holy Spirit.

Here are some illustrations of the way in which, for St. Paul, unity is bound up with basic elements in the gospel. First, he will have known something of the teaching Jesus gave to his disciples that they are to be a fellowship of humility, love and service, *because* they are his disciples. Secondly, Jesus had given himself completely in total self-sacrifice. His followers must therefore not live for themselves (*2 Cor.* 5: 14ff.). If they are in Christ and share in the Spirit there must be no quarrelling and self-glorification among them; on the contrary, they must consider the interests of others and not their own, because the divine Christ humbly took human form and status and died obediently the death of the cross (*Phil.* 2: 1–11). His self-abnegation is the pattern for Christian humility and love among believers. This inner quality of the unity of Christians in a common life is well summed up in a passage like *Colossians* 3: 9–15. But the points made in these and similar passages are never far from St. Paul's mind, whatever he is speaking about.

But St. Paul has more explicit things to say about what unites Christians into a community or Church. It is not simply that they believe alike and are kind and charitable to one another. In *Galatians* 3: 26, 27, 28, he says we are all sons of God through faith in Christ Jesus. "For those who were baptized into Christ put on Christ." And so, he goes on to say, racial and social distinctions no longer count; "you are all one in Christ Jesus". Our unity in Christ is based on faith in Christ and baptism into Christ, and in this unity the things which divide men are overcome.

The profound nature of this unity is further shown in *1 Cor.* 12. In the new translation verses 12 and 13 run, "For Christ is like a single body with its many limbs and organs, which many as they are together make up one body. For indeed we were all brought into one body by baptism, in the one Spirit, whether we are Jews or Greeks, whether we are slaves or free men, and that one Holy Spirit was poured out for all of us to drink." So Christ's body is one, it is entered by baptism, its members participate in one Holy Spirit, who distributes among the members differing gifts which contribute to the life of the one organism (verses 14–26). Christians are not simply, as one might say, "a body or group of people"; they are *Christ's* body and each of them members or limbs of it (verse 27). This teaching is repeated in summary in *Rom.* 12: 3–6. In Christ, then, Christians are united in a common relationship to him and to one another, and all share in the "communion of the

Holy Spirit" (*2 Cor.* 13: 14). Their unity comes from beyond themselves; it is more than human goodwill and brotherhood; they are joined together in and by the living Christ by the operation of the one Spirit in the many members of the body. To be in Christ means for St. Paul to be a member of the visible community of believers which is his body.

There is one other striking reference in *1 Cor.* to a basic element in Christian unity, in chapter 10, verses 16, 17. The apostle is speaking of the bread and cup of the Eucharist. "The bread which we break, is it not the communion of the body of Christ? Because there is one bread, we who are many are one body, for it is one bread of which we all partake." So the apostle sees Christians being made into one body, because they all partake of one bread, which is the communion of the body of Christ. They have a unity which comes from their common participation in the eucharistic bread.

What we have seen in detail is summed up in *Ephesians* 4: 3-6, in which the key words we have noticed are brought together. "There is one body and one Spirit, as there is also one hope held out in God's call to you; one Lord, one faith, one baptism; one God and Father of all, who is over all and through all and in you all."

We may put the points about unity in St. Paul's teaching in the order in which we have met them in these notes in the following way:

1. St. Paul's *apostolic ministry* exercised personally and through his authorized delegates kept the local Christian congregations together in one Church.

2. The *sacred books* of what we call the Old Testament were everywhere read and revered by Christians. Later on St. Paul's letters, the four gospels and other books were put together to form the New Testament and so complete the Christian Bible. Then as now the Scriptures were common ground and a point of unity among Christians.

3. St. Paul was clear that as there is one God so there is one Lord, Jesus Christ, and one gospel of which he is the centre. Scattered through the epistles are many short summaries of *this faith* which Christians accept as the basis of their common life in Christ and in the Spirit.

4. Christians enter on their new life by professing their faith in *baptism*. They are baptized into Christ and his body, the Christian community, and receive the Holy Spirit, in order to live together the common life of which Christ is the source and the pattern.

Their unity in Christ is expressed and renewed by receiving together the one bread of the *eucharist,* which is the communion of Christ's body.

This is a summary of the particular features of the unity of the Church as we have discovered them in St. Paul's letters. In the two or three centuries after the apostle's death, the Church found by experience that these features of its life were indeed the focal points of its unity and identity as the Church of Christ. They remain so today, and the movement towards unity must take them all into account.

CHAPTER XI

ST. PAUL IN HISTORY

by

T. M. Parker

TO understand the impact of St. Paul upon the later history of the Church it is necessary to remember that even in his own day the Roman Empire consisted of two parts, the Western, Latin-speaking, half and the Eastern, where Greek was the *lingua franca*, a division which was eventually to lead to the two worlds of the Middle Ages, Western Christendom and Byzantine Christendom, which had been growing apart for a long time and by the end of the Middle Ages were in ecclesiastical schism from each other. St. Paul himself was by origin very much a man of the Eastern Roman world, who wrote in Greek and thought in terms of Greek rather than Latin culture. Moreover he was a Jew, whose education was at Jerusalem, where he sat at the feet of the famous Rabbi Gamaliel. His knowledge of rabbinic theology is very apparent in his letters. In his own words he was "circumcised the eighth day, of the stock of Israel, of the tribe of Benjamin, an Hebrew of the Hebrews; as touching the law, a Pharisee; concerning zeal, persecuting the church; touching the righteousness which is in the law, blameless" (*Phil.* 3: 6–7), what we should call today an Orthodox Jew. His conversion to Christianity, although it made him regard the Judaism of his youth very differently, did not alter his way of seeing theology; his approach to it is very rabbinic and often he can be understood only if we remember this. Later ages were apt to forget that when, for example, St. Paul contrasts faith and works, the "works" of which he is speaking are primarily "the works of the Law", i.e., exact obedience to the Torah, the Law of Moses, not just good deeds in general.

On the whole, then, it is surprising that this very Eastern man was to have more effect on Western church history than in the East. Yet so it was. Paul was read and commented on in the East, of course, but, broadly speaking, it was Western theologians who cultivated him most. It may be that the clear-cut mind of St. Paul, logical and legalistic by training, appealed to the Roman mind, the greatest achievement of which was the Roman Law, still in many ways the foundation of modern legal systems. Several of the Latin Fathers had a legal background—Tertullian and Cyprian, for example, and the greatest of them, St. Augustine, though not himself a lawyer, had been a teacher of rhetoric, occupied before his conversion in teaching young men how to present legal arguments in court attractively and forcefully.

And it was St. Augustine who, more than any other of the earlier Latin theologians, based his teaching very much upon Pauline theology. And St. Paul, though by no means uninterested in the mystical aspect of Christianity, was one who naturally set much store by the moral side of his new religion, once again a preoccupation of the Western Christian mind, and saw Christianity very much as a way of life, often putting union with God and Christ in the background. Like all generalizations this is an oversimplification, but it is this aspect of the Western Church which is all important in understanding the Western attitude to St. Paul. And this brings in the whole question of grace, which ever since the time of St. Augustine has been a central and hotly debated matter in Western theology and was ultimately to be the problem which lies at the root of the great division in the West between Catholicism and Protestantism, a division which lies not so much in matters of sacramental theology, ceremonial, the priesthood and so on, but upon different understandings of how man is saved by Christ.

It is important here to understand that at the heart of the dispute lies, as so often, a question of translation, for East and West, as we have seen, talked different languages. The word translated in our English bibles as "grace" occurs very frequently in the Pauline epistles. But the Greek word he actually used, *charis*, meant to him the unmerited favour which God shows us by saving us through Christ and the Holy Ghost. The word used to translate it in the Latin Bible is *gratia*, from which the English word "grace" derives. And to St. Augustine in particular, this meant the divine help by which alone we are able to live the Christian life, and, since St. Augustine had and continues to have an almost overwhelming influence upon Western theology, this is what it means in virtually all Western Christian thought. St. Paul, of course, believed that God's aid was needed to give Christian faith and life, of which man is incapable by his own efforts, but he expresses it ordinarily by the word *pneuma*, spirit, meaning thereby primarily the work of the Holy Spirit upon man's soul. Broadly speaking this is the way in which Greek Christian theology has looked upon what in the West we call "grace" ever since, although it has also insisted upon the work of the Holy Spirit in uniting us to the Humanity and Godhead of God the Son. To anticipate a little, this attitude to grace was also present in the medieval Western schoolmen, especially in the one whose famous *Sententiae*, Peter Lombard, became from the twelfth century onwards the textbook of medieval schoolmen, upon which all the theological students in the universities were obliged to lecture and comment, and he identified grace with the Holy Ghost. This, however, did not prevent medieval theologians from criticizing and even denying Peter Lombard's view of grace and thus there sprung up a distinction between the Holy Spirit as "uncreated grace" and "created grace", which they looked at as an endowment of all baptized Christians set up in the soul by uncreated grace, which in turn led some of them to think of grace as almost a "thing" in itself, caused by God, but made the possession of man. Hence the constant criticism of the medieval West, by both Easterns and Protestants, as having made grace something impersonal, rather than the influence of God upon the soul.

To return, however, to St. Augustine. Since he regarded grace as the Divine force acting upon man's will, thus straying away from St. Paul's understanding of his word *charis*, and since it is very evident that the greater part of mankind are either non-Christians or bad Christians, he saw the giving of grace as something arbitrary, given or not given to individuals as decided by God, thinking of it in terms of predestination. God chose, from the *massa peccati* which mankind had become since the Fall, relatively few to receive faith and grace, "passing over" the majority and thereby dooming them to eternal loss, and this for no merit or demerit of their own, but ultimately because of their involvement in the sin of Adam, original sin, which he thought of as not merely a weakness but blameworthy in his descendants, who were potentially in Adam when he fell. This was the core of his argument with Pelagius (who, interestingly enough, was of British or Irish origin), and thought that original sin was the result of the imitation of Adam, not of the heritage which his descendants received from him.

It is this fact which brings the doctrine of predestination, which was to be such a storm centre in Western theology, into the picture. If God arbitrarily chose those to whom he would give grace, as St. Augustine thought, then clearly he must have decided this in the distant past (in so far as we can think of past and present in connexion with God) and thus predestinated some to be saved and others to be lost. St. Augustine never went quite as far as to make God the author of sin, but his teaching on predestination, which became more and more stark towards the end of his life, came very near it. It was this implication of St. Augustine's thought which the Church decisively rejected at the Council of Orange in 529, which, though affirming much of St. Augustine's teaching, said "But not only do we not believe that some have been predestinated to loss by the divine power, but also, if there be any who will believe so evil a thing, we say to them, with all detestation, anathema".

So, stark Augustinianism, or what it seemed to imply, was never fully endorsed by the Church, great as was to be Augustine's authority for all later Western theologians. Towards the end of the Middle Ages there was indeed a movement away from Augustinianism, especially on the part of the followers of William of Ockham, the great English theologian of the fourteenth century, who founded a school of thought which was to be influential, if not dominant, all over Western Christendom. The Ockhamists were accused by their opponents of being at least Semipelagians and indeed some of their views did approach Pelagianism, as when they said that grace was necessary for salvation only because God had chosen that it should be, not because of man's helplessness without God, or claimed that by living a good life by means of his own resources, man could actually *deserve* that God should give him grace.

It was against this teaching that Luther revolted, even though by theological training he was himself an Ockhamist, and in many of his other views always remained so. To him it was intolerable that man could in any way merit salvation or even that he should play any personal part in its process. God and God alone saved man, and it was in this sense that he understood St. Paul, whose epistles, he once said, contained more gospel than the written gospels themselves. St. Paul, as interpreted by Augustine, was the very centre of his teaching. But he went further still. Instead of thinking of grace as a curative force acting upon man, he thought of it as the legal act by which God chose to acquit man of responsibility for original and actual sin in the process of "justification", by which God initially removed man from the state of sin to that of a saved being. (He did not deny a later sanctification of man, as God enabled him to love God and do good works, but denied that man's love for God played any part in the initial process of justification, yet he opposed the teaching of some of his extreme followers, the Antinomians, who denied the law of God played any real part in the Christian life, which seemed to mean that, provided man retained faith, he could live as he liked and yet attain final salvation. But man to Luther never played any real part in his salvation, except by "saving faith", that is by becoming aware of the love of God displayed in the crucifixion of Christ. This is the famous Lutheran doctrine of "salvation by faith *alone*", which Luther sometimes described as the gospel itself and certainly thought of as the very centre of Christianity in the light of which all else was to be understood, as is the case with strict Lutherans today. To Luther grace was merely a drug, which suppressed the symptoms of sin, not a strengthening food which enabled man to cast it off.

It is important, however, to realize, as some of his opponents (notably our own Thomas More) did not, that by faith Luther did not mean bare intellectual faith, accepting the truth of the Creed. Rather he meant the kind of faith by which man puts all his trust in God, *fiducia* (as when we "believe *in* someone"), which, though he himself would have denied it, seems to involve at least some degree of love of God. He did not think of man as saved by any initiative of his own, for even saving faith was, he emphasized, itself the gift of God, which could in no way be attained by man's own efforts, still less deserved.

We see here once again the influence of the doctrine of predestination, though it is fair to point out that Luther, like Augustine, derived this from St. Paul, who not only speaks of Christians as predestinated "unto the adoption of children by Jesus Christ to himself, according to the good pleasure of his will" (*Eph.* 1: 5-6), but also, in the *Epistle to the Romans* graphically speaks of God as making of the same clay both "one vessel unto honour, and another unto dishonour" (*Rom.* 9: 21), which would seem to imply predestination not only to salvation but also to eternal loss. Many have overlooked the fact that St. Paul in *Romans* puts forward this argument as one possible reason for the fact which he, as a Jew, found so inexplicable, the rejection of Christ, the Messiah, by his own chosen people, and this is only a preliminary to his final conclusion that God permitted the Jews to apostatize in order that the Christian Church might turn to the evangelization of the Gentiles, and its success with them would impress the Jews and eventually bring them too to Christ, "and so all Israel shall be saved" (*Rom.* 11: 26). Predestination, even if it plays a part in St. Paul's thought, is far from being the predominant element in it, as the sixteenth century Reformers seem almost to have thought. Because all of them were minimizers of the part played by man in salvation, predestination, which seemed to rule out any possibility of man's being the master of his fate and the captain of his soul, naturally appealed to them. Calvin here merely put more systematically and scientifically what had been said by Luther (for instance in his reply to Erasmus's plea for freewill, boldly entitled by Luther *De servo arbitrio*). Indeed it has been pointed out that to Calvin, although he has gone down in history as the Apostle of Predestination, that doctrine was by no means the centre of his theological system, which was far more the sovereignty of God, from which predestination seemed to follow as a necessary consequence.

But it would be a great mistake to think that the Protestants were the only predestinarians of the sixteenth century. Many medieval theologians had been no less predestinarian. In fact Archbishop Bradwardine of Canterbury in the fourteenth century had attacked those theologians of his day whom he believed to be Pelagians, in his *Contra Pelagianos,* which was so uncompromising in its attack upon any real co-operation of any human freewill in salvation, that centuries later his book was reprinted by extreme Calvinists as a good exposition of their own position. St. Thomas Aquinas, too, is predestinarian in his views, a fact which I find often surprising to Roman Catholic pupils, who think of predestination as a purely Protestant invention. Nor did this cease to be the case after the Reformation. It is curious to find that predestination and freewill were topics which proved divisive in Roman Catholicism in the later sixteenth and in the seventeenth century. It began with Baianism, which originated at the University of Louvain in the mid-sixteenth century and was the precursor of Jansenism, which rent the French Church in the seventeenth century, and had much influence elsewhere. Two schools of thought had, in fact developed, the predestinarian, especially prominent in St. Thomas Aquinas's order, the Dominicans, and systems which gave more scope to human freewill and were developed by the Jesuits, notably in their prominent theologian, Molina. This division of opinion led to the lengthy hearing at the papal court of the arguments placed before the *Congregatio de Auxiliis*, which, after going on many years (1597-1607) at the turn of the sixteenth and seventeenth centuries, ended inconclusively with a mere papal exhortation to both sides to abstain from controversy and a refusal to condemn either view. All this was in the end to give rise to the even greater Jansenist controversy, in which at first both sides equally tried to gain the ear of the Papacy, although in the long run Jansenism, which claimed to follow St. Augustine to the letter, was condemned.

It is curious that these disputes are very much paralleled by similar controversies in the Protestant Churches. After Luther's death his great friend and helper, Melancthon, was accused of teaching Synergism, the view that human freewill and co-operation played *some* part in the process of salvation, and these and other topics caused great controversies between the supporters of Melancthon and the Gnesio-Lutherans ("genuine Lutherans"), as they called themselves, and were brought to an end only by the *Book of Concord* (1577-1580), an immensely long document which is still one of the official formularies of Lutheranism. Later it was the turn of the Calvinists, in the controversy between the Arminians, who rejected Calvin's view that the eternal fate of all men was fixed long before their creation and known from all eternity before the Fall, which was in a sense contrived by God as an excuse for damning those he had from all eternity resolved to damn. It is even more remarkable that these parallel controversies went on more or less contemporaneously without apparently influencing each other at all—so much had the Reformation isolated Catholics and Protestants—a fact that to my mind suggests that, as I hinted before, some characteristic of the Western European mind, perhaps its addiction to logic, impels Western Christians to an absorbing interest in the questions of freedom, determinism and grace. What is even more surprising is the ardour with which these battles, from the fifth century down almost to our own time, were fought and the degree to which men could accept what often seem to us degrading ideas of God not merely with reluctant assent but with enthusiasm.

It is perhaps curious and sad that St. Paul, the great apostle of Christian unity and unanimity in Christ, gave rise unconsciously to what we have seen to be the most persistent and often most bitter dispute in the Western Christian Church. It is almost an example of the proverbial saying that:

"The evil that men do lives after them;
The good is oft interred with their bones."

Not that St. Paul did any conscious evil by his writings; it is rather that, like many great men, he could neither foresee nor prevent what later generations would make of his thought, once they had forgotten its historic background and failed to see the paradoxes which inevitably entwine themselves in the writings of really great men.

INDEX

Abraham, 93, 121
Achaia, 41, 46, 50, 53, 59, 65, 68, 70, 76
Achaicus, 53, 61
Acts of (the) Apostles, 17, 20, 22, 37-42, 56-57, 64, 76 n. 51, 80, 87, 90, 115
Acts of Paul and Thecla, 17, 75, 90 n. 4
Acts of St. Paul, 37, 66 n. 39, 75, 77
Acworth, Angus, 73
Adam, 127
Adders, 83, 84
Adriatic Sea (Adria), 47, 73 n. 47, 82, 83, 84
Aegean Sea, 23
Agape, 118
Agrippa I (Marcus Julius Agrippa, King Herod in *Acts* 12), Tetrarch of Ituraea, etc., 68
Agrippa II, King (Marcus Julius Agrippa), King of Chalcis, Tetrarch of Ituraea, etc., 70, 71
Aldersgate Street, 11
Alexandria, 19, 43
Allen, Roland, 52, 77
Amplias, 53
Anamnesis, 117
Ananias, 20, 32, 59
Andronicus, 53
Antinomians, 129
Antioch (Pisidian), 22, 34, 46, 54, 59, 62
Antioch (Syrian), 21, 22, 25, 42, 43, 44, 45, 46, 53, 59, 60, 62, 63
Antony, Mark (Marcus Antonius), Roman Triumvir, 67
Apelles, 53
Apocalypse (Revelation), 51, 52, 77, 116
Apollos, 51 n. 23, 53, 61, 64, 112, 119
Apostles, 28-30, 39
Appii Forum, *see* Forum of Appius
Aquae Salviae, 28
Aquila, 41, 49, 51 n. 23, 53, 61, 64
Aquilo, 73 n. 47
Aquinas, St. Thomas, *see* Thomas, St., Aquinas
Arabia (Arabia Petraea), 20, 33, 42
Aratus, 56 n. 27

Archippus, 54
Areopagus, 56
Aristarchus, 75
Arminians, 131
Artemis, 25, 61
Asia (Roman province), 23, 27, 51, 63, 65, 76
Asia Minor, 80
Assos, 46, 49
Asyncritus, 53
Athene, 97
Athens, 19, 46, 53, 56, 59
Attala, 46
Augustine, St. (of Hippo), 104, 126, 127, 128
Augustus (Caius Julius Caesar Octavianus), Roman Emperor, 66, 71

Baianism, 130
Baptism, 107-114, 123
Bar-Jesus, 62 n. 30
Barnabas, St., 21, 22, 23, 32, 43, 44, 45, 46, 54, 55, 60, 62, 63
Barrett, C. K., 87 n. 1
Benjamin, 125
Bernice (Berenice), sister and consort of Agrippa II, 70
Beroea, 46, 53, 59
Bible, 90, 123
Bithynia, 65
Bornkamm, G., 39, 43 n. 13, 47 n. 19, 78
Bradwardine, Archbishop, 130
"Bridge" terms, 107
Brundisium (Brindisi), 73 n. 47
Bunyan, John, 102
Byzantine Christendom, 125

Caesarea, 25, 26, 34, 46, 47, 49, 69, 74, 80
Calvin, John, 101, 104, 130, 131
Carpenter, S. C., 16
Castor and Pollux, 81
Cauda (Clauda), 82
Cenchreae, 46, 58
Cephas (Peter), 21, 112
Charismatic movement, 101
Charles V, 79
Chase, F. H., 54 n. 25

133

Chios, 46
Chloe, 61
Church, 54, 114, 116, 118, 119-124
Churchill, W. S. (Sir Winston Churchill), 30, 57
Cicero, 18, 67
Cilicia, 19, 43, 60, 65, 67
Circumcision, 19, 45, 119, 125
Clark, A. C., 42 *n.* 12
Claudia, 54
Claudius (Tiberius Claudius Nero Germanicus), Roman Emperor, 41, 44 *n.* 15
Claudius Lysias, 49, 67, 69
Clement (? St. Clement of Rome), 53
Clement of Rome, St., 75
Cleopatra, 67
Clermont-Ganneau, C. S., 65 *n.* 34
Codex Bezae, 42
Codex Sinaiticus, 101
Colossae, 52
Colossians, St. Paul's writings to the, 52, 74, 89
Colossians, Epistle to the, 25, 61, 120, 122
Constantine, 77
Constantine Porphyrogenitus, 79, 84
Coos, 46
Corinth, 13, 23, 24, 26, 41, 46, 49, 50, 52, 53, 55, 56, 58, 59, 61, 68, 76, 87, 99, 116, 119, 121
Corinthians, 16, 101, 112
Corinthians, Epistles to the, 60-61, 88, 89, 95, 100, 115, 116, 118, 122, 123
Crete, 47, 73 *n.* 47, 76, 80
Crispus, 53, 55
Cydnus, 67
Cyprus, 44, 46, 52, 62, 63, 65, 80
Cyrene, 44
Cyril of Jerusalem, St., 76

Damascus, 11, 12, 13, 20, 31, 32, 34, 43, 49, 64
Dante, 71
Demas, 54
Demetrius, 61, 70
Demre, 80
Derbe, 46, 59
Diaspora (Dispersion), 19, 22, 66 *n.* 39, 109
Dion Cassius, 41 *n.* 11
Dittenberger, W., 41 *n.* 8
Dix, Dom Gregory, 116, 117
Doddridge, Philip, 103
Dominicans, 130

Domitian (Titus Flavius Domitianus), Roman Emperor, 77
Donne, John, 90
Dubrovnik, 84

Ecumenical movement, 119
Election, doctrine of, 16
Elizabeth I, Queen of England, 97
Elymas, 62 *n.* 30
Epaenetus, 53
Epaphras, 52, 53, 64, 75
Ephesians, 61, 98
Ephesians, Epistle to the, 25, 74, 89, 98, 100, 123
Ephesus, 23, 24, 25, 46, 51, 53, 55, 56, 60, 63, 70
Epicureans, 56
Epilepsy, 35
Erastus, 53, 58, 76
Eubulus, 54
Eucharist, Holy, 88, 115-118
Euodias, 53
Euraquilo, 73 *n.* 47, 82, 83
Euroclydon, 73 *n.* 47, 82
Europe, 39
Eurus (Euros), 73 *n.* 47, 83
Eusebius, 77

Fair Havens, 47, 76 *n.* 52, 80, 81
Faith (in theology), 103, 129
Fall, 131
Felix, Antonius, 50, 68
Festus, Porcius, 69-70, 80
Flood, 113
Foakes-Jackson, F. J., 41 *n.* 8
Foinikias (Phoenika), 81
Fortunatus, 53, 61
Forum of Appius (Appii Forum), 47
Fourth Crusade, 84
Francis, St. (of Assisi), 11
Francis Xavier, St., 36
French Church, 130

Gaius, 53, 58
Galatia, 22, 23, 46, 59, 65
Galatians, 60
Galatians, Epistle to the, 23, 32-33, 44, 59, 88, 89, 93, 119
Gallio, Lucius Junius, 41, 53, 68, 87
Gamaliel, 19, 122
Genesis, 98
Gentiles, 21, 22, 29, 33, 44-45, 54, 55, 66, 74, 79, 97, 100, 118, 119, 121
Gnesio-Lutherans, 131
God-fearers, 55

Grace, 97-106
Grace abounding, 102
Grace in the New Testament, 97
Greece (see also Achaia), 23, 25
Greeks, 100

Haenchen, Ernst, 38 n. 2, 49 n. 21, 50 n. 22, 78
Harnack, A., 38 n. 2
Headlam, A. C., 16
Hebrews, Epistle to the, 64, 85
Hellenists, 19, 32, 33, 34
Hermas, 53
Hermes (companion of St. Paul), 53
Hermes (Greek god), 57, 62
Herod Agrippa, *see* Agrippa I
Herod the Tetrarch, 46
Herodion, 53
Hetoimos, 62
Hickling, C. J. A., 89 n. 2
Hierapolis, 52
Holy Eucharist, *see* Eucharist, Holy
Holy Roman Empire, 71
Homer, 97
Hooker, M. D., 89 n. 2

Iconium, 22, 46, 53, 59, 75
Illyricum, 24, 65, 73
India, 38, 83
Infant baptism, 113-114
Irenaeus, 76
Isaac, 121
Isaiah, 110
Italy, 49 n. 20, 80

James, St. ("brother of the Lord"), 29, 38, 43, 45
James, St. ("the Great", son of Zebedee), 28, 44, 76 n. 51
Jansenism, 130, 131
Jason, 53, 55, 59
Jeremiah, 117
Jerusalem, 19, 21, 22, 23, 26, 28, 32, 33, 43, 44, 45, 46, 49, 50, 70, 77, 80, 120
Jerusalem, Council of, 22, 44, 45, 59, 63
Jesse, Branch of, 108
Jesuits (Society of Jesus), 53, 130
Jesus Christ, Lord, 14, 16, 20, 22, 26, 32, 34, 35, 41 n. 11, 43, 45, 51, 56, 70, 71, 74, 88, 92, 99, 100, 106, 108, 109, 110, 111, 117, 118, 120, 121, 122, 131
Jesus Justus, 54
Jews, 25, 45, 51, 54, 55, 56, 80, 93, 116

John, St. ("the Evangelist", son of Zebedee), 28, 38, 44, 63
John the Baptist, St., 51 n. 23
John Mark, *see* Mark, John
Jonah, 113
Josephus, 49 n. 20
Judaea, 20
Judaizers, 23
Julia, 53
Julius, 80
Junia, 53
Justification, 16, 100, 128
Justus, 55

Kenilworth, 97
Kingdom of God, 108
Kingsley, C., 43
Kipling, Rudyard, 83
Knights of St. John, 79

Lake, Kirsopp, 41 n. 8
Laodicea, 51, 52, 61
Laodiceans, 61
Laodiceans, Epistle to the, 61
Last Supper, 88, 116, 117
Latomus, 105 n. 9
Law (in theology), 101, 102, 105
Law, Roman, 126
Lebanon, 80
Lex Julia, 66, 68 n. 43
Linus, 53, 76
Lloyd George, D. (1st Earl Lloyd-George of Dwyfor), 39, 57
Lokrum, 84
Lord's Prayer, 112
Louvain, 130
Lucina, 77
Lucius, 53
Lucius of Cyrene, 46, 90
Luke, St., 15, 26, 40, 42, 45, 53, 56, 61, 64, 66, 70, 73, 76, 80, 82, 83, 85
Lukinos, Cape, 82
Luther, Martin, 105, 128, 129
Lutherans, Lutheranism, 131
Lycia, 65
Lydia, 49
Lystra, 22, 46, 57, 59, 62, 66 n. 39

Macedonia, 23, 25, 36, 46, 50, 59, 65, 70, 76
Malta (*see also* Melita), 73, 79, 80, 82, 83, 84
Manaen, 46
Mark, John, St., 53, 63, 76
Mark Antony, *see* Antony, Mark
Mary, Blessed Virgin, 51 n. 23

Mary of Rome, 53
Matthew, St., 90
Mediterranean Sea, 36, 64, 82
Melancthon, 131
Melita (Melite) *(see also* Malta, Mljet),* 47, 73, 79, 81, 83
Meriamlik, 75
Messina, Straits of, 81
Meteorological Office, 81
Methodist movement, 12
Miletus, 46, 56, 77
Mitton, C. L., 99, 103
Mljet *(see also* Melita), 73, 79, 80, 82, 83, 84
Moffatt, James, 97, 102
Molina, 130
Morton, H. V., 77
Moses, 111, 117, 121, 125
Mozley, J. K., 98
Muggeridge, Malcolm, 77, 91 *n.* 5, 92 *n.* 7
Muratorian Canon, 38 *n.* 1
Myra, 47, 80
Mytilene, 46

Nabataeans, 43
Nereus, 53
Nero (Nero Claudius Caesar Augustus Germanicus), Roman Emperor, 27, 75
Neronian persecution, 47 *n.* 19, 77
New English Bible, 109
New Testament, 98, 101, 104, 113, 115, 116, 119
Newman, J. H., 43
Newton, John, 103
Nicopolis, 76
Nymphas, 54

Ockham, *see* William of Ockham
Odysseus, 97
Odyssey, 97
Old Testament, 98, 104, 107, 113, 121
Olympas, 53
Onesimus, 52, 54, 74, 75, 94
Onesiphorus, 75
Orange, Council of, 128
Orontes, 21, 53
Orosius, 41
Ostia, 77

Palestine, 26, 47 *n.* 19, 67
Pallas, 68
Pamphylia, 46, 65
Paphos, 62
Papias, 63 *n.* 31

Parthia, 38
Passover, 51, 116-117
Pastoral epistles *(see also Timothy, Epistles to; Titus, Epistle to),* 27, 76
Patara, 46
Patrobas, 53
Paul, St.
  Birthplace, 14, 17, 19, 34, 43, 50, 67, 92
  Parentage and early life, 19, 50, 125
  Jewish name Saul, 19, 62-63, 64
  Latin name, 64-65
  At stoning of Stephen, 12, 20, 31
  Conversion, 11-14, 31-35, 125
  Period after conversion, 32-34, 42-44
  First missionary journey, 46, 54, 62, 63, 65, 75
  Second missionary journey, 46, 55, 58, 59, 60, 63, 65-66
  Third missionary journey, 46, 49, 56
  Arrest in Jerusalem and trial, 66-71
  Appeal to Caesar, 69-71
  Voyage to Rome and shipwreck, 37, 71-74, 79-84
  Two-year stay in Rome, 74-75
  Last years, 75-77
  Execution, 37, 77
  His methods of travel, 49
  His craft of tent-making, 49-50
  His collections for "the saints", 50-51
  His letters, 13-14, 17-18, 20, 23, 24, 37, 39-40, 53, 57-61, 76, 85-96, 124, 126
  His speeches, 56-58
  His claim to be an Apostle, 28, 29, 30, 120
  Apostle to the Gentiles, 11-16, 106
  His personality and uniqueness, 15
  On Baptism, 107-114
  On the Holy Spirit, 107-114
  On the Holy Eucharist, 115-118
  On Grace, 97-106
  His personal appearance, 17, 58-59, 67 *n.* 41, 96
  Imprisonments, 25, 40, 46, 47, 66-67
  Roman citizenship, 66-68
Paulus (of Crete), 64 *n.* 33
Paulus (4th cent. jurist), 68 *n.* 43
Pelagianism, 128, 130
Pelagius, 127

Pentecost, 60
Pentecostal movement, 101
Perga (Perge), 46, 63
Pergamos, 51
Perowne, Stewart, 9, 77, 83
Persis, 53
Peter Lombard, 127
Peter, St., 28, 33, 37, 38, 43, 44, 45, 60, 119
Peter, Epistles of St., 38 *n.* 2, 61, 86
Peter's Pence, 44
Pharisees, 19
Phenice, *see* Phoinika
Philadelphia, 51
Philemon, 53, 74, 75, 94
Philemon, Epistle to, 25, 74, 75, 94, 95
Philip ("the Deacon"), 36
Philippi, 23, 46, 49, 50, 53, 65, 66 *n.* 40
Philippians, Epistle to the, 25, 74, 89, 92
Philologus, 53
Phlegon, 53
Phoebe, 53, 58
Phoenicia, 44
Phoenika (Phenice), 80, 81, 82
Phrygia, 46, 65
Pompey (Gnaeus Pompeius Magnus), Roman Triumvir, 67
Pontus, 65
Porcius Festus, *see* Festus, Porcius
Pozzuoli (Puteoli), 47, 73, 81, 82
Praetorian Guard, 74
Predestination, 127-128, 129-130
Priscilla, 41, 49, 51 *n.* 23, 53, 61, 64
Prophecy, 109
Ptolemais, 46
Ptolemy (Claudius Ptolemaeus), 73 *n.* 47
Publius (Poplios), 73
Pudens, 54
Puteoli (Pozzuoli), 47, 73, 81

Quartus, 53, 58

Raleigh, Sir Walter, 97, 98
Ramsay (Sir) W(illiam) M., 38 *n.* 2, 40, 44 *n.* 16, 73, 77
Real Presence, 88
Reformation, 104, 130
Reformers, 105
Reggio di Calabria *see* Rhegium
Renan, E., 92 *n.* 7
Resurrection (of Jesus), 34
Revelation, *see Apocalypse*

Revised Standard Version, 101
Rheglum (Reggio di Calabria), 47, 73, 81
Rhodes, 46, 79
Richard I (Richard Coeur de Lion), 84
Robinson, J. Armitage, 98
Roman Catholic Church, 43, 105
Roman Catholicism, 130
Roman church, 43
Roman Empire, 15, 23, 54, 64, 71, 88, 125
Romans, 71
Romans, Epistle to the, 24, 34, 37, 58, 88, 89, 95, 100
Rome, 26, 27, 38, 43, 46, 47, 49 *n.* 20, 50, 53, 56, 70, 71, 73, 77, 79, 89, 105, 119
Rosenthal, F., 65 *n.* 34
Rufus, 53

St. Andrew-by-the-Wardrobe, 11 *n.*
St. Mark, Gospel of, 98
St. Matthew, Gospel of, 98
St. Paul, *see* Paul, St.
St. Paul's Bay, 80
St. Peter, *see* Peter, St.
St. Peter, Basilica of, Rome, 10
SS. Peter and Paul, Feast of, 38
Salmone, 80
Samos, 46
Samson, 108
San Paolo fuori le mura, Basilica of, Rome, 77
Sanday, W., 16
Sanhedrin, 32, 59
Sardis, 51
Schoolmen, 105
Scott, Sir Walter, 97
Scythia, 38
Seleucia, 21, 75
Sencourt, Robert, 92 *n.* 7
Seneca (Lucius Annaeus), 41
Seneca, Marcus Annaeus, 41 *n.* 9
Sententiae (of Peter Lombard), 127
Septuagint, 19, 98
Sergius Paulus, 62, 64, 65
Sherwin-White, A. N., 41, 42, 67 *nn.* 41 and 42, 70 *n.* 46, 78
Sicily, 73
Sidon, 47, 80
Silas (Sylvanus), 53, 59, 63, 64, 66
Simeon (Niger), 46
Sin, 102
Smith, James, 80, 82, 83
Smyrna, 51
Sosipater, 53
Sosthenes, 53, 68

137

Spain, 27, 70
Spirit, Holy (Holy Ghost), 25, 46, 65, 107-114, 122, 123, 126-127
Stachys, 53
Stephanas, 53, 61, 113
Stephen, St., 12, 20, 31, 38, 44, 45
Stoics, 56, 92
Suetonius, 41 *n.* 11
Synagogue(s) 43, 54, 66 *n.* 39, 109, 121
Synergism, 131
Syntyche, 53
Syracuse, 47, 73 *n.* 47, 81, 82
Syria, 43, 60, 65, 67
Syrtes, Great, 73 *n.* 47

Tarsus, 14, 17, 19, 34, 43, 50, 67, 92
Tertius, 53, 58, 94
Tertullian, 76, 77
Thecla, 66 *n.* 39, 75 *(see also, Acts of Paul and Thecla)*
Theophilus, 64
Thessalonians, Epistles to the, 59, 89, 108, 109
Thessalonica, 46, 53, 55, 59
Thomas, St. (Apostle), 38
Thomas, St., Aquinas, 105, 130
Three Taverns, 47
Thucydides, 37, 57
Tiber, 53, 77
Timothy, St., 51, 53, 59, 60, 64
Titus, St., 45, 53, 60, 64
Titus, Epistle to, 76, 113
"Tongues", 109

Toomer, G. J., 65 *n.* 34
Torah, 125
Troas, 46, 49, 76
Trogyllium, 46
Trophimus, 54, 66, 76
Tryphena, 53
Tryphosa, 53
Turks, 79
Twelve, The, 29
Tychicus, 53
Tyrannus, 49, 55
Tyre, 46

Ulpian, 68 *n.* 43
Underhill, Evelyn, 13
Urbane, 53

Valerian persecution, 77
Vatican, 88
Vatican Council, Second, 101
Via Appia, 73 *n.* 47, 81
Vidler, Alec, 77, 91 *n.* 5, 92 *n.* 7

Wade-Gery, T. H., 57
Wesley, Charles, 102
Wesley, John, 11
Western Christendom, 125, 126, 128, 131
Western text, 42, 55 *n.* 26, 62 *n.* 30
William of Ockham, 128
Works (in theology), 102, 125

Zenas, 54